Light Through a Prism

Light Through a Prism

Social Justice Teaching for Refugee and Displaced Students

Terri L. Rodriguez; Laura Mahalingappa; Ayan Amoud Omar; Lauren Ergen; Odeese Ghassa-Khalil; and Jennifer L. Meagher;

ROWMAN & LITTLEFIELD
Lanham • Boulder • New York • London

The research reported in the (book, article, or monograph) was made possible (in part) by a grant from the Spencer Foundation (#Spencer 202000177). The views expressed are those of the authors and do not necessarily reflect the views of the Spencer Foundation.

Published by Rowman & Littlefield
An imprint of The Rowman & Littlefield Publishing Group, Inc.
4501 Forbes Boulevard, Suite 200, Lanham, Maryland 20706
www.rowman.com

86-90 Paul Street, London EC2A 4NE

Copyright © 2024 by Terri L. Rodriguez, Laura Mahalingappa, Ayan Amoud Omar, Lauren Ergen, Odeese Ghassa-Khalil, and Jennifer L. Meagher

All rights reserved. No part of this book may be reproduced in any form or by any electronic or mechanical means, including information storage and retrieval systems, without written permission from the publisher, except by a reviewer who may quote passages in a review.

British Library Cataloguing in Publication Information Available

Library of Congress Cataloging-in-Publication Data

Names: Rodriguez, Terri, 1967- author. | Ghassa-Khalil, Odeese, author. | Meagher, Jennifer, L. author. | Omar, Ayan Amoud, author. | Ergen, Lauren, author. | Mahalingappa, Laura, 1975- author.
Title: Light through a prism : social justice teaching for refugee and displaced students / by Terri L. Rodriguez, Odeese Ghassa-Khalil, Jennifer L. Meagher, Ayan Amoud Omar, Lauren Ergen and Laura Mahalingappa.
Description: Lanham, Maryland : Rowman & Littlefield, [2024] | Includes bibliographical references. | Summary: "Light Through a Prism explores stories of K-12 educators committed to social justice pedagogy, especially with refugee and displaced students, as they navigate the complexities of pandemic-era schooling"— Provided by publisher.
Identifiers: LCCN 2023053794 (print) | LCCN 2023053795 (ebook) | ISBN 9781475870589 (cloth) | ISBN 9781475870596 (paperback) | ISBN 9781475870602 (ebook)
Subjects: LCSH: Children of immigrants—Education—United States. | Refugee children—Education—United States. | Social justice—Study and teaching—United States. | Culturally relevant pedagogy—United States. | Critical pedagogy—United States. | COVID-19 Pandemic, 2020—Influence. | Teachers and community—United States. | Teaching—Social aspects—United States.
Classification: LCC LC3746.R63 2024 (print) | LCC LC3746 (ebook) | DDC 371.826/9120973—dc23/eng/20240110
LC record available at https://lccn.loc.gov/2023053794
LC ebook record available at https://lccn.loc.gov/2023053795

This book is dedicated to refugee and displaced children who enter schools in their new homes with open minds and hopeful hearts every day. And to their teachers, who shine a light and make a difference.

Contents

Foreword	ix
Introduction	1
Chapter 1: Issues Surrounding Refugee and Displaced Students	11
Chapter 2: Critical Consciousness and White Saviorism in Teacher Narratives	21
Chapter 3: Changemaking and Resisting	37
Chapter 4: Empathy and Agency	51
Chapter 5: Vulnerability and Overcoming Challenges	69
Chapter 6: Building Classroom Community and Advocacy	87
Chapter 7: Recommendations for Supporting Educators of Refugee and Displaced Students	107
Index	119
About the Authors	121

Foreword

What scholars choose to write about is powerful. The texts we read can reinscribe reality and limit what we see as possible. We also live up to the dystopias or utopias we imagine and share out loud. Thus, we can write and read our way into the world we want to see and into the teaching force our children need to thrive. We need more stories of teachers who move mountains for children who experienced forced displacement and sought refuge in the United States. We need more scholarship that draws teachers' eyes to portraits of aspirational peers, so they can look closely and catch inspiring glimpses of their own reflections.

Instead of detailing what teachers are not doing and what has not worked, forward-thinking scholarship highlights what successful teachers are doing and doing well (e.g., Boutte, 2022; Gonsalez et al., 2006; Ladson-Billings, 2022; Lee, 1993; Long et al., 2016; Nash et al., 2022; Wynter-Hoyte et al., 2022). The same systems that choose to portray teachers as incompetent tend to see children as broken and incomplete, which could not be further from the truth.

Children who experienced forced displacement come to our classrooms with wholeness and fullness across a range of ways of knowing, being, and doing (Nash et al., 2022). They are in the United States to live fully, fearlessly, creatively, joyfully; to dream up possibilities and envision potentialities—to live far beyond a minimum basic standard of physical safety (Espiritu et al., 2022). *Light Through a Prism* offers a teacher-affirming look at the dedicated labor of social-justice oriented educators who tirelessly work with such children.

The authors of the book draw readers into a much-needed space of seeing teachers in their daily efforts to live up to the honor and responsibility of playing a part in the dreams of the children who fled dangerous legacies of colonialism and imperialism, oppressive governments, targeted violence fueled by racism, religious extremism, etc. As we look at the unique stories of the teachers across different contexts and classrooms, we see many sides of a prism that together tell a fuller story of *who*, *why*, and *how*. We see three-dimensional portraits of teachers who aspire.

Speaking of *who*, the teaching force is not a monolith; no two teachers are alike. At the same time, classrooms serving the children are inherently and infinitely multicultural and multilingual. Social-justice–oriented educators recognize that no one teacher can represent all their students' identities and speak all their languages. Instead of aching for the ease of often deceitful similarity, they continuously embrace the desire to make it about the students: seeing the classroom for who the children are and creating a space where all belong.

Educators learn from their children, families, communities, and available resources. Humility and productive discomfort of not knowing today is their "fuel for tomorrow." Teachers also aim to understand how racism, nationalism, classism, ableism, monolingualism, heteronormativity, etc. impact their children's and their own experiences. Powerful depictions of successful teachers showcase their processes of getting to know the children in their fullness and carefully considering one's own interpretational lenses.

Portraying *why* effective educators choose to teach channels and directs collective action. Often regarded as a rewarding profession, teaching gives us something in return for our hard work. The familiar desire to "make a difference" resonates with teachers for a reason. Fulfilment often comes from being a part of something bigger. Social-justice–oriented teachers aim to make a difference by challenging systems that underserve children. In doing this work, they must also actively examine and challenge teaching calls framed by omnipotent damaging narratives surrounding refugee flight.

These discourses often pull teachers to feel as though they are rescuers of the needy, broken, lacking, and incomplete—to embody "compassionate domination" (Ong, 2003, p. 47). Often mistaken for a lens of empathy, such a lens creates a craving for the gratitude of the saved to profoundly affirm the rightness of the saviors and their worldview, and the lack of such gratitude fuels backlash (Espiritu et al., 2022). Social-justice–oriented educators see children's strengths and their full humanity with humility and profound respect. Their *why* is the joy of seeing students learn deeply and live fearlessly despite inequities in education that they both face.

Scholarly teacher portraits must also highlight the *how*, showcasing procedures of teaching as a contextual interpretive process that works for their students (e.g., Hollins, 2015; 2019). When learners are at the center, teachers reject supposedly universal "best practices" that continue to fail the same groups of students. They observe children's responses to learning experiences, interpret these responses, and translate their observations to practice through continuous cycles towards deeper learning, drawing on admirable levels of professional knowledge and personal agency.

Social-justice–oriented teachers resist assimilationist pressures and affirm students' identities through culturally relevant (Gay, 2018) and sustaining pedagogies (Paris & Alim, 2017). They create curricular spaces for family and community memory, incorporating art, poetry, oral storytelling, music, and other forms of creative expression that brought families pride and joy before displacement and will be passed down to new generations in exile.

Teachers develop students' critical consciousness by collectively working to understand oppressions and histories that cause displacement worldwide and to see how nations and people heal and rebuild. They work in solidarity toward a world where humanitarian injustices anywhere are a shared responsibility of humankind to be resolved and prevented.

Finally, children and teacher successes are deeply intertwined. All of us, educators or not, play a role in shaping the aspirational sociocultural and political *where*. Reading *Light Through a Prism* invites a reflection and consequential dialog on how we can build a nation where aspiring teachers succeed. What do societies that support teachers do? What do school systems that take care of teachers look like? How do policies show that they value teachers' professional expertise and agency? After all, if we want to see children live fully, we need to support their teachers wholeheartedly.

By Ekaterina Strekalova-Hughes

REFERENCES

Boutte, G. S. (2022). *Educating African American students: And how are the children?* Taylor & Francis.

Gay, G. (2018). *Culturally responsive teaching: Theory, research, and practice.* Teachers College Press.

González, N., Moll, L. C., & Amanti, C. (Eds.). (2006). *Funds of knowledge: Theorizing practices in households, communities, and classrooms.* Routledge.

Hollins, E. R. (2015). *Culture in school learning: Revealing the deep meaning* (3rd edition). Routledge.

Hollins, E. R. (2019). *Teaching to transform urban schools and communities: Powerful pedagogy in practice.* Routledge.

Ladson-Billings, G. (2022). *The Dreamkeepers: Successful teachers of African American children* (3rd edition). John Wiley & Sons.

Lee, C. D. (1993). *Signifying as a scaffold for literary interpretation: The pedagogical implications of an African American discourse genre.* National Council of Teachers of English.

Le Espiritu, Y., Duong, L., Vang, M., Bascara, V., Um, K., Sharif, L., & Hatton, N. (2022). *Departures: An introduction to critical refugee studies*. University of California Press.

Long, S., Souto-Manning, M., & Vasquez, V. (Eds.). (2016). *Courageous leadership in early childhood education: Taking a stand for social justice*. Teachers College Press.

Nash, K. T., Arce-Boardman, A., Peele, R. D., & Elson, K. (2022). *Culturally sustaining language and literacy practices for Pre-K-3 classrooms: The children come full*. Teachers College Press.

Ong, A. (2003). *Buddha is hiding: Refugees, citizenship, the New America*. University of California Press.

Paris, D., & Alim, H. S. (Eds.). (2017). *Culturally sustaining pedagogies: Teaching and learning for justice in a changing world*. Teachers College Press.

Wynter-Hoyte, K., Braden, E. G., Myers, M., Rodriguez, S., Thornton, N., & Boutte, G. (2022). *Revolutionary love: Creating a culturally inclusive literacy classroom*. Scholastic.

Introduction

This book is intended for educators, and those who care about the educational outcomes, of a particularly vulnerable group of students in US schools. When children who have experienced forced displacement from their homes enter schools in new and faraway places, they bring with them a host of strengths, opportunities, hopes, and dreams. They also bring memories and experiences of the traumatic events that dislodged them. Some travel with their families, while others travel alone.

Educators are in a unique position to foster supportive relationships and positively influence these children's lives. They can practice pedagogical love and play a central role in helping refugee families develop empathy, solidarity, and trust with one another as well as with the children's classmates and themselves (Wilkinson & Kaukko, 2019). Teachers can advocate for the pedagogical practice of critical love—a profound and ethical commitment to caring (Sealey-Ruiz, 2022). This is important because compassion and love play an important role in refugee educational resettlement.

The teachers highlighted in this book view schools as places of healing and hope. At the same time, they know that school systems are ill-equipped to respond to these children's specialized needs. They recognize that negative schooling experiences impact their students' lives and futures (Strekalova & Hoot, 2008; Wang, Strekalova-Hughes, & Cho, 2019). Yet they continue to reach out, day after day, with aspirational intentions to make a difference.

The authors came together as career educators to celebrate and explore the experiences of classroom teachers who work tirelessly to support their students. Together, the authors and teacher participants generated shared narratives of the successes and struggles they encountered in striving to create socially just classroom environments. Unplanned, as it was for all, the COVID-19 pandemic intervened in the research and shaped the narratives that were emerging. The authors describe this shared work as a prism that invites multiple perspectives and many truths about the experiences of the teachers featured here.

PRISM AS A METAPHOR: SHEDDING LIGHT ON THE ISSUES

As narrative inquirers, the authors find the prism metaphor useful. Through it, they are able to appreciate how narrative inquiry affords new ways of looking at teacher identity, practice, and experience. When light shines through the plane faces in the triangular pyramid, it is separated into a spectrum of colors. The systematic light of narrative inquiry shines through the angled faces of the prism, or the shared generated stories, and illuminates the work. Light is refracted to make the spectrum visible—in other words, the spectrum of color is always present, but not visible, in the light.

Metaphorically, new understandings are possible—they are, in a sense, already present. In this way, solutions to problems related to refugee educational resettlement can be made visible with new questions and new methods of study that come from many different angles. The "truths" that emerge don't stand by themselves as individual, unrelated realities—they can be envisioned as a whole truth. This book is an attempt to flesh out the myriad of ways that many truths can be leveraged to better support refugee and displaced students.

NARRATIVE INQUIRY AND PORTRAITURE

The teachers' stories were gathered and studied using a research design called narrative inquiry. Narrative methodologies are well-suited to understanding how teachers' experiences inform their beliefs and constructions of professional identities and practices. Connelly and Clandinin (1999) contribute the term "personal practical knowledge" to describe the ways in which teachers draw on past experiences to craft teaching identities and practices.

The authors share professional identities as social-justice–oriented teachers with extensive experience supporting refugee and displaced students. They come together from different geographic regions, contexts, roles, and life experiences. Two, including a Somali-American and a Syrian-American researcher, share the linguistic, ethnic, and racial identities of many of their former refugee and displaced students. This is important because, like teaching, research is both personal and professional. The authors' identities and experiences inform the work as interpretive analytic tools.

Alongside narrative inquiry, the authors employ a technique called portraiture (Lawrence-Lightfoot & Davis, 1997). Each chapter offers case studies of several teachers, studies that are designed to capture the richness, complexity, and dimensionality of the teachers' experiences while conveying their perspectives. In all, the authors invite readers to consider, with a listening heart and an open mind, the stories of ten experienced classroom teachers.

Each portrait is developed through multiple interview dialogues between the researcher and the participant. The authors work with both light and shadow to bring each portrait to life. In other words, while they celebrate the teachers and their stories, they bring a critical lens that may appear at times to reflect teachers in unflattering ways. Like all human stories, neither those of the authors or the teachers are perfect or complete. Our stories always carry our shadows, for, without them, we could not appreciate the light.

PARTICIPANTS AND RESEARCHERS

The teachers live and work with students who are from refugee or displaced backgrounds and who have been resettled in two geographic regions in the United States. The first chapter lays a foundation for understanding the schooling experiences of these children in general in the past decade. Subsequent chapters feature case-study portraits of teachers who generously shared their time, wisdom, and great hopes for themselves and their students.

In each chapter, the authors present a found poem from the interview data to introduce the participant. Found poems are arrangements of interview data—in other words, words are selected from the interview transcripts and are the words of the participants' themselves. Because the authors asked teachers to share about themselves, and also to make their interpretive intentions explicit, the authors thought it only fitting that they, too, construct poems about themselves and their backgrounds. The authors next each introduce themselves through a poem about themselves and a short biography.

Terri

I am from cold and snow/And flat black earth/That in the spring/Turns green in perfect/Symmetrical/Rows of corn./I am from Wally and the Beav'/And June and Ward—/That family who lives/In the dark-brown/Suburban style/Ranch./I am from rough farmer's hands/And grandma's cheek/Made smooth with/Oil of Olay/And the wearing of hats/In the sun.//I am from/Lefse at Christmas/And tater tot hotdish./Mashed, au gratin, fried, riced,/And a million other ways to eat/Potatoes.//I am from don't talk much/Shake hands. (No hugs.)/From "Hey, girlie."/And a quarter/Held enticingly forth/To a grandchild/Who will learn/To save.

Terri is a former classroom teacher, a teacher educator, and an educational researcher. She self-identifies as a White, English-speaking, Christian, able-bodied, cisgender woman. She has lived and taught in many different parts of the world. She was raised in a suburban city in the Midwest where she has returned to work with preservice teachers. Her interests in supporting teachers of refugee and displaced students are both personal and professional as she comes full circle "home" to find it a very different place than when she left more than thirty years ago.

Lauren

I'm only thirty years old./I've only lived in [name of state]./I only know English./White, middle class, female//I've only taught in one building./I've only taught high-school students.
I've only taught multilingual learners./An undergraduate degree in English Language Arts and Teaching English as a Second Language/A Master's degree to underscore my investment, priority, belonging:/Students from strong educational backgrounds/and other students with a wealth of diverse experiences/Paths that lead them to the same classroom./

For their first exposure to English//I am a dichotomy between ten years of valuable experience:/focused on language acquisition holistically/English language arts or English language development,/they can be one in the same/focused on newcomer English learners/I'd rather tell you about "who" I teach than "what"/the curriculum is guided by individual skills/focused on those with limited or interrupted educations.//Education is a fundamental human right.//Developing home languages and English simultaneously/and colleagues with triple the number of years of service I've put in./(but, I'm not close to finished with my work).

Lauren brings the perspective of a classroom teacher. She teaches refugee and displaced students in their first and second year after arriving in the United States. She is a White, monolingual English speaker who continues to reside in the same midwestern state in which she was raised. As a college student, Lauren learned about the refugee populations arriving in her city. An early volunteer tutoring experience sparked her interest in working with English learners. From the onset of Lauren's career as an educator, she found a home with multilingual learners in a large high school. She earned an M.A. in Teaching English as a Second Language (TESL).

Lauren notices how her identities and background in many ways create a barrier between herself and her students. Especially because Lauren knows only English, she aspires to be observant and creative about ways to connect with her learners. She strives to incorporate more diverse perspectives and linguistic plurality in the materials she uses to teach and the ways she supports and assesses learners. Lauren is interested in this project because it is an opportunity to examine the powerful ways educators reflect and develop their practice in order to advance the support and celebrations multilingual students deserve.

Odeese

I come from a distance from a different world./Fitting within the box until my tongue twirled./I had a lot to share but knew no words to say/Afraid to be ridiculed . . . so, humbly, I prayed/I came/to climb mountains of books; they look so strange./In a world of maybe(s)? . . . impossible? . . . in range?/To realize discomfort is fuel for tomorrow./To reach for the stars so their light we borrow/As one, we emerge from darkness into day./To celebrate togetherness in every way.

Odeese currently works as a community consultant. She immigrated to the United States in the early 1990s as a young adult and faced various obstacles while pursuing post-secondary education. Despite many barriers, she earned her bachelor's, master's, and doctorate degrees in education while assisting family members in relocating and building lives in the United States. She has witnessed and experienced many life-changing events as a daughter, mother, student, educator, and active member of society.

Although she met personal computers at the age of twenty-four, she later designed a fully online Arabic-language-and-culture bachelor's degree program, teaching Arabic to non-Arabic speakers. Her professional life has come full circle through her small business, a cross-cultural language training company supporting non-English speakers, specifically students and families of refugee and displaced backgrounds. She has conducted cross-cultural presentations and workshops to highlight the importance of social tolerance in society.

Jennifer

I am from/Two homes, two lives/The city, the lakes and fields/All/High expectations/Service to others/Driven to succeed/Faith and family/Courage and discipline//I am from/Gram's rough nurturing hands/Grandpa's silver dollars/Mom's embracing of difference/Dad's get-r-done and have fun attitude/Family first, blood calls us together
Loving and helping others is what we do//I am from/Wednesdays and Sundays at church/Summers Up North/The suburbs, the city, the small town'/ The country, the rez, places yet/to be known/Wanderlust and old book dust/ The call to learn and grow//

I am from/The seat/looking out the window/Miles on the road and in the air/Observing, exploring, absorbing,/Connecting then creating/My own place on this journey/To who I will be and/where I will eventually leave from.

Jennifer is a former school administrator and classroom teacher who currently works in teacher education. She is a wife, mother, teacher, leader, lifelong learner, and community member who identifies as White, Christian, and Scandinavian. Born, raised, and always living in the same rural midwestern state, Jennifer recognizes the stereotypes around the geography related to her home and identity; however, those stereotypes have been dismantled throughout her experience. She earned degrees in English and secondary education, curriculum and instruction, secondary-school administration, and educational leadership.

Throughout her career, Jennifer has endeavored to lead with love and understanding. Her personal and professional learning has been centered on educational improvement, whether that be ways to teach writing, include diverse voices in secondary classrooms, engage and assess students, or build advocacy in students and staff. These interests intersected in this research as Jennifer explored how teachers perceive their own agency and build it in their students.

Ayan

I am dual/I am at the same time and same space/I am a world far away and in between/I am a Black woman, but not Black enough in America/I am a refugee, but not refugee enough in America/I am a generation after, but close enough to know better/I am a Black educator, attuned to my Blackness/I am a Somali-Muslim educator, balancing eclectic truths//I am my mother, a quiet movement/I am my mother, a survivor/I am my mother, the Northern Star and an anchor/I am my mother, an oral tradition of folktales//

I am a mother of two girls, a conscious and/determine upward motion/I am a recipient/Of that metaphorical first page/A representation of possibilities and a constant foreboding of impossibilities/I am the product of twelve in a family/living in a three-bedroom two-bathroom apartment//

I am The seat at the table, an invisible weight/I am Do I really belong here, or am I an imposter/I am Are you my child's language arts teacher?/I am Do you speak English?/I am Where are you REALLY from?/I am How long have you lived in America, your English is so good//I am my name, mispronounced and all/I am/learning endurance through my mother's bifocals/I am a diverse growing community/An articulate question that is desperate/An intentional decision that is loaded//Most importantly,/I am belonging/I am a teacher/I am for students/All of our students.//And,/I am a continuation.

Ayan is a district equity coordinator and a former classroom teacher. She is a Somali-Muslim American refugee living in the United States since 1993. She grew up in the rural South, spending most of her young life immersed in Black culture, which shaped much of her future goals. A pursuit of higher education led her to the Midwest, where she completed her master's degree with an emphasis on Black literature, specifically the works of Toni Morrison.

In the affair of learning and teaching, Ayan found a platform that allowed her to listen to others and share her personal, educational, and professional journey. She applies her literary passion, using the power of storytelling and narrative inquiry, to counter the fear-mongering rhetoric stirred by the aftermath of 9/11 and continued in more recent political events, such as the 2021 Capitol attack. Her powerful narrative includes a recollection of her refugee experience, finding hope, and the continuous journey to success.

Laura

I am a mix of cultures/that coalesced in a land of steel and coal/Samosas and lasagna/the staples of my household//Subsistence farmers/Factory worker/Union man
Doctor/Nurse//Warriors and pacifists/Lofty thinkers and salt of the earth// Risk takers and comfort seekers/All contributed to the rights of my birth// My people are loud but warm/Fond of sports but not athletic/Sometimes judgmental/though it's meant to be helpful//What are you?/A question often received, hard to answer/A person, a daughter, mother, sister, wife, friend/I am a whole from a mix that made me who I am

Laura is a former language teacher and a current teacher educator and researcher. She grew up multiracial in America and identifies as a South Asian/White, multilingual woman. Raised in northeast, rural America, she personally experienced being "diverse" in K–12 public schools in the United States. She experienced high expectations from teachers while at the same time being stereotyped by them. She also learned how to negotiate her multifaceted identity in many different ways. She uses critical perspectives to help work and advocate for marginalized students.

CHAPTER SUMMARIES

The first chapter provides a general overview of educational outcomes, issues, and challenges for refugee and displaced students in the United States. It includes recent trends in the field and the needs of students in schools. The chapter also presents the foundations of theories and frameworks that guide the research and are further explicated throughout the other chapters.

In the next chapter, "Critical Consciousness and White Saviorism in Teacher Narratives," the authors delve into the contradictory ways that White teacher narratives demonstrate aspirations toward critical consciousness while also embodying aspects of White saviorism. It explores the narratives of two White, suburban, midwestern, public-high-school teachers. Chloe, an English as a second language (ESL) teacher, and Jill, an English language arts (ELA) teacher, narrate their passionate convictions around their roles supporting refugee and displaced students. Both demonstrate a keen sense of self-awareness.

The third chapter presents the experiences of two educators, Elizabeth and Kaylee, who both talk about themselves as makers of and resisters to change. Their classrooms are in a suburban, midwestern high school. They teach in a new-to-country program, which is part of a school-within-a-school model, where students begin their education journey in the United States. This chapter focuses on the ways that Elizabeth and Kaylee narrate the practices and perspectives that create a welcoming learning space for newcomer learners.

In the fourth chapter, entitled "Empathy and Agency," the authors explore how empathy and agency are visible in the narratives of two rural, midwestern, public-school teachers. Steven is a history teacher, and Naomi is an ESL teacher. This chapter focuses specifically on their work with Puerto Rican students displaced by Hurricane Maria in 2017. Within a diverse community marked by culturally complex relationships, the authors highlight the role of critical self-reflection and the importance of dismantling barriers.

The chapter entitled "Vulnerability and Overcoming Challenges" explores vulnerability and the ways in which two urban, northeastern public-school teachers, Emily and Nicole, overcome challenges as ESL teachers. The authors argue that it is, indeed, these teachers' vulnerability that fosters their abilities to creatively overcome a myriad of challenges, especially during the COVID-19 pandemic.

In the final narrative chapter, entitled "Building Classroom Community and Advocacy," the authors offer portraits of two public-school teachers, Kay and Janet. Kay is a retired, suburban, elementary music teacher while Janet is a veteran teacher of ELA in an urban high school. The authors argue that Kay and Janet are equity-literate educators of refugee students and that their stories demonstrate unique approaches to community building and advocacy in and out of the classroom.

The book concludes with a reflective chapter entitled "Critical Hope and Healing." In this chapter, the authors join voices to weave together themes and to reiterate the lessons learned during a global pandemic. They offer recommendations for educators at all levels. The authors hope to leave the reader with a vision of educators as justice warriors and activists who, every day, welcome and affirm every child into their lives, their classrooms, their schools, and their communities.

REFERENCES

Connelly, F. M., & Clandinin, D. J. (Eds.) (1999). *Shaping a professional identity: Stories of educational practice. Teachers College Press.*
Lawrence-Lightfoot, S. & Davis, J. H. (1997). *The art and science of portraiture.* San Francisco: Jossey-Bass.
Sealey-Ruiz, Y. (2022, May). An Archaeology of self for our times. *English Journal, 111*(5), 21–26.
Strekalova, S. & Hoot, J. L. (2008). What is special about special needs of refugee children?: Guidelines for teachers. *Multicultural Education, 16*(1), 21–24.
Wang, C., Strekalova-Hughes, E., & Cho, H. (2019). Going beyond a single story: Experiences and education of refugee children at home, in school, and in the community. *Journal of Research in Childhood Education, 33*(1), 1–5, DOI:10.1080/02568543.2018.1531670.
Wilkinson, J., & Kaukko, M. (2019). Educational leading as pedagogical love: The case for refugee education. *International Journal of Leadership in Education, 23*(1), 70–85.

Chapter 1

Issues Surrounding Refugee and Displaced Students

Schools are experiencing massive shifts in student populations due to widespread global crises and migrations of people. Thus, for several decades, the field of education has focused on teachers' knowledge and skills to work with students whose backgrounds and experiences differ from theirs. Over a decade ago, a prominent teacher educator wrote:

> If one were to name an issue that can be found near the top of the list of crucial topics within the critical education literature, it would be *globalization* ... [E]ducation cannot be understood without recognizing that nearly all ... policies and practices are strongly influenced by an increasingly integrated international economy that is subject to severe crises; that reforms and crises in one country have significant effects in others; and that immigration and population flows from one nation or area to another ... impacts ... what counts as official knowledge, [and] what counts as a responsive and effective education (Apple, 2007, p. 223).

Among students in the United States affected by these immigration and population flows, refugee and displaced students are a particularly vulnerable group with unique education needs.

It is well understood that teachers are a decisive element in seeking to transform educational inequities through socially just teaching. Teachers frequently lack the necessary knowledge and skills to address the needs of these students, partly because teaching outside of the comforts of their own schooling experiences leaves them feeling vulnerable (Ukpodoku, 2007). However, research affirms that paradigm shifts can occur in teachers' beliefs, knowledge, and skills when intentional conversations and interactions centered in community formation become the focus of professional development (Croce, 2018).

Teachers who question their own biases and examine deficit views can reimagine their own and refugee and displaced students' strengths, skills, and needs to improve instruction (Mosselson, 2006). Teachers can navigate increasingly complex curricular demands, design inclusive instruction with limited resources, and relate in caring ways with students whose backgrounds and experiences are far-removed from their own.

This chapter provides a general overview of educational issues and challenges for refugee and displaced students in the United States. First, it presents who refugee and displaced students are and their particular needs in today's schools. It then explains the theories and frameworks that guide the project and how these shape what the authors can and cannot see and know. Through socially just teaching, it frames the needs of teachers and students.

REFUGEE AND DISPLACED PEOPLES

The United Nation's Office of the High Commissioner for Refugees (UNHCR, 2023) estimated that the number of people displaced from their homes has reached over 103 million worldwide. Among these, 32.5 million are *refugees*, which is a legal designation for displaced people who left their home countries to "escape persecution or a serious threat to their life, physical integrity or freedom," because of their race, religion, nationality, political beliefs, or membership in a social group but also due to "situations of conflict, violence or public disorder" (UNHCR, 2023). Approximately half are children, with six million being of school age.

In contrast, people who are *internally displaced* relocate to a different area within their countries. People within a country are displaced for a variety of reasons, including economic issues, environmental degradation and climate crises, and political instability. In the United States, there have been two recent examples of climate emergencies, including communities being displaced from New Orleans by Hurricane Katrina and from Puerto Rico by Hurricane Maria. In many cases, roughly twelve to sixteen percent of displaced people in the United States do not return to their homes long-term, which means that they do not return within six months or remain away permanently.

The US government grants a certain number of people per year refugee status based on eligibility criteria and an extensive vetting process. They often prioritize the most vulnerable populations, such as individuals from conflict areas or those with young children (Dryden-Peterson, 2016; Immigration Research Initiative, 2023). Since 1975, millions of refugees have resettled in the United States. They have come from many different countries all over the world due to various crises, which change over time (Krogstad, 2019).

The number of refugees that the United States welcomes each year is dependent on administration priorities—under the Trump administration, for instance, only 12,000 arrived in 2020, while under the Obama administration in 2016, the United States resettled around 85,000. Biden has set the 2023 target as 125,000. Over the past decade, refugees to the United States have originated from Myanmar, Iraq, Bhutan, Democratic Republic of Congo, Somalia, Iran, Syria, Cuba, and Ukraine.

SOCIALLY JUST TEACHING FOR REFUGEE AND DISPLACED STUDENTS

Social-justice–oriented teaching is informed by critical multicultural education (Grant & Sleeter, 2006); culturally relevant teaching (Ladson-Billings, 2006); and equity literacy (Gorski & Swalwell, 2015). These fields offer insights into teachers' ways of "doing" and "being" (Ladson-Billings, 2006, p. 41). Equity literacy synthesizes goals of multicultural education and culturally relevant teaching while decentering culture.

In addition to highlighting how teachers "do" social-justice pedagogy, Swalwell (2013) describes the "activist ally" teacher as one who is "intent upon facilitating the development of justice-oriented citizens with a deep understanding of systemic injustices, a sense of agency that is empowered and critically self-reflective, and the ability to mobilize their resources in order to act in concert with others" (p. 108). This stance is crucial for the education of refugee and displaced students.

Children living in refugee and displaced families have unique needs as a student population. Educators, including administrators, teachers, counselors, and paraprofessionals, should be aware of cultural and language barriers, psychological stresses such as PTSD, issues related to limited or interrupted schooling, and potential discrimination, especially based on current sociopolitical contexts (McBrien, 2005). Many of these students "have witnessed or directly experienced unimaginable violence and suffering as they and their families sought safety and refuge here in the United States" (Mendenhall & Bartlett, 2018, p. 109).

Apple (2007) warns teachers not to view refugee and immigrant youth as passive victims, though, but rather to position them as active agents. Affording refugees the chance to articulate and share their visions for their future could enable schools to shift perspectives about students' capabilities and design programs and curricula that support learners in achieving their goals (Daniel, 2019, p. 81). Social-justice–oriented teaching should focus on students' voice and their multiple identities and perspectives.

Admittedly, social-justice teacher development unfolds in rich and complex ways. There is no single framework or pedagogy that is more likely than another to foster it; rather, naming oneself a social-justice educator implies that one has taken a stance that seeks to "notice and name inequities, disrupt hierarchies of power and privilege, and interrupt . . . practices that reproduce injustices" (Conference on English Education, 2009). A need exists to conduct in-depth studies of teacher learning toward social justice (Cochran-Smith & Zeichner, 2005).

CULTURALLY RELEVANT TEACHING

Culturally relevant teaching is an educational approach that can foster social-justice–oriented teaching. It emphasizes the importance of incorporating students' cultural backgrounds, experiences, and identities into the teaching and learning process (Ladson-Billings, 2006). The goal is to create an inclusive and equitable learning environment where all students can thrive academically and personally. Culturally relevant teachers aim to create educational experiences that are meaningful and empowering for students, helping them develop a positive self-identity while also preparing them for success in an increasingly diverse world.

Culturally relevant teaching involves student-centered learning where the curriculum reflects the cultural backgrounds of refugee and displaced students. This inclusive curriculum may incorporate texts, literature, historical events, and examples from their cultures and perspectives. It recognizes that students learn best when they can connect the curriculum to their own lives. Teachers should provide opportunities for students to share their cultural experiences and perspectives, and they should engage students in active and meaningful learning experiences that relate to their lives.

Building positive and respectful relationships with students is also essential. Teachers should create a classroom environment where students feel valued, safe, and respected, regardless of their cultural backgrounds. Involving parents and the broader community in the educational process is another aspect of culturally relevant teaching. This can include engaging parents from diverse backgrounds in the classroom, seeking their input, and recognizing the value of their cultural knowledge (Aronson & Laughter, 2016).

Critical Perspectives and Teachers

Culturally relevant teaching often incorporates critical pedagogy (Kincheloe, 2008), which encourages students and educators to think critically about social issues, power structures, and inequalities. It empowers students to become active participants in their own education and advocates for social justice. Culturally relevant teaching responds to equity and social justice by going beyond just acknowledging cultural diversity; it aims to address systemic inequities in education. Teachers should work to create equitable opportunities for all students, ensuring that no one is disadvantaged due to their cultural background.

By taking a critical perspective, teachers may engage in critical consciousness-raising (Freire, 1974/2021) activities. Critical consciousness-raising involves the development of an awareness of societal power dynamics, injustices, and the need for social change. This concept, for instance, is applied to the representation of refugees, encouraging individuals to question and analyze how refugees are portrayed in various contexts. It seeks to challenge and dismantle biased or oppressive narratives that may perpetuate stereotypes, discrimination, or misinformation through interrogation of narratives in public discourse.

Consciousness-raising can help teachers understand how dominant ideologies develop and function as tools for dominant groups to shape the consciousness of marginalized groups to maintain an oppressive system that perpetuates social inequalities. Through critical consciousness-raising, preservice teachers can question the dominant ideologies imposed upon them by critically analyzing how education for refugee and displaced students is structured and how they can help push back against any barriers to success and work towards these students' liberation.

RefugeeCrit

The study also employs refugee critical race theory (RefugeeCrit) as a specialized theoretical framework necessary for reframing experiences and informing education praxis (Strekalova-Hughes & Nash, 2017). RefugeeCrit has foundations in critical race theory and provides tools and strategies for investigating relations between people in social institutions like schools (Vargas, 2003).

RefugeeCrit merges legal studies with multicultural education and foregrounds personal experience; the linguistic and cultural identities and practices of students and teachers; and the social, historical, economic, and political contexts within and outside classrooms. RefugeeCrit emphasizes a nuanced perspective through the lenses of critical consciousness and critiques against white saviorism. Through critical consciousness-raising, teachers perceive the positionality of refugees and the need for agential voices and counternarratives and storytelling (Delgado & Stefancic, 2000) to counter colonial and racist mentalities (Strekalova-Hughes, 2019).

This framework also acknowledges that the experiences of refugees are shaped by various intersecting factors, such as gender, ethnicity, race, religion, and socioeconomic status. It calls for an intersectional analysis to understand how these identities impact refugees' experiences. The framework seeks to deconstruct stereotypes and oversimplified representations of refugees, emphasizing their diversity, resilience, and capacity for self-determination.

The social construction of race also intersects with legal refugee status and geographic spaces, affecting students' sense of belonging and citizenship within those identities. Intersectional identities shape students' experiences in varying social contexts. Thus, teachers should avoid essentialism to strive for a critical understanding of refugee experiences and complex identities (Strekalova-Hughes, 2019).

RefugeeCrit also challenges the prevalent trope of the "White savior" in educational efforts. The phenomenon of White saviorism can reinforce and validate historical inequities to ultimately validate White privilege (Anderson, 2013). RefugeeCrit critiques narratives where White or Western individuals are portrayed as heroes who rescue or save refugees, often perpetuating a colonialist and paternalistic perspective. It highlights the importance of centering the voices and agency of refugees themselves, rather than perpetuating a top-down, colonialist approach to addressing refugee issues.

Critical race theory (CRT) and RefugeeCrit aim to go beyond merely critiquing representations and narratives. They call for advocacy and action to address the structural issues and policies that contribute to the displacement of people and the challenges they face. While critical, these perspectives also encourage empathy and solidarity with refugees. It recognizes the importance of connecting with the humanity of refugees and acknowledging their shared experiences and aspirations, ultimately supporting action for positive change and social justice for refugees.

Teacher Action and Refugee Students

Included in critical consciousness-raising and culturally relevant teaching is the idea that teachers first need to become aware of their own cultural biases and then become open to learning about the diverse cultural backgrounds of their students. This includes understanding the cultural norms, values, traditions, and histories that shape students' lives. Teachers should be sensitive to the cultural differences and experiences of their students. This includes avoiding stereotypes or biases in classroom materials and interactions.

Teachers engage in ongoing self-reflection and professional development to enhance their cultural competence and teaching practices (Gorski & Dalton, 2020). By engaging in critical self-reflection, teachers can move away from acritical perspectives to critical ones, where they perceive unjust social power structures, investigate their causes, and visualize and enact alternatives and challenges to the status quo (Gay and Kirkland, 2003).

Critical, deep self-reflection is important for teachers of marginalized students. Critical reflection calls on individuals to consider various aspects of their identities and how their either privileged or marginalized statuses affect the teaching. In her work, Sealey-Ruiz (2022) promotes an "archeology of self" that promotes racial literacy and requires teachers to interrogate their ideas and biases to work toward change. It requires teachers to have a profound ethical commitment to care and advocate for all students, especially those who are refugees and displaced.

Teachers should thus have empathy for students, understanding their experiences and viewpoints, which begins with understanding their own. Through the vulnerability and humility of being open to self-examination, teachers can understand the limits of their own worldview (Sealey-Ruiz, 2022). It can further develop into considering contextual and historical forces that perpetuate systemic inequities and social injustice.

Teachers' effectiveness in working with students requires intention and desire to act. Teacher agency (Priestley et al., 2015) can develop into advocacy for refugee and displaced students. Work towards culturally relevant teaching, social justice, and equity must be done individually and in community for it to have the influence and power needed. In schools, this process can be particularly challenging with the presence of institutional barriers that push against teacher agency. Teachers should be empowered in their work to develop their skills and knowledge and apply them to their support of refugee and displaced students.

Current professional development may not adequately attend to teachers' knowledge and skills related to social-justice teaching in support of refugee and displaced students. Cochran-Smith (2003) argued almost two decades ago that a problem in social-justice teacher preparation is an inability to fully account for the "unforgiving complexity of teaching" (p. 3). Teacher education for social justice remains a contested idea because "it is viewed as prioritizing progressive and political goals at the expense of traditional academic learning goals" (Cochran-Smith, Gleeson & Mitchell, 2010, p. 35).

Overall, it is important to expand our knowledge of effective approaches to the education of refugee and displaced students. Considering the important role of teachers in student success, it is important to understand how we can better prepare and guide teachers in their work with this vulnerable population. It is essential that we investigate teachers' current views about and experiences in working with refugee and displaced students. The more we recognize effective and essential approaches of teachers who have had substantial experience supporting these students, the better prepared we would be to support all teachers.

REFERENCES

Apple, M. W. (2007). Global crises, social justice, and teacher education. *Journal of Teacher Education, 62*(2), 222–34.

Aronson, B., & Laughter, J. (2016). The theory and practice of culturally relevant education: A synthesis of research across content areas. *Review of educational research, 86*(1), 163–206.

Cochran-Smith, M. & Zeichner, K. (2005). *Studying Teacher Education: The Report of the AERA Panel on Research and Teacher Education.* Routledge/Taylor and Francis.

Cochran-Smith, M. (2003). The unforgiving complexity of teaching: Avoiding simplicity in the age of accountability. *Journal of Teacher Education, 54*(1), 3–5.

Cochran-Smith, M., Gleeson, A. M., & Mitchell, K. (2010). Teacher education for social justice: What's pupil learning got to do with it? *Berkeley Review of Education, 1*(1), 35–61.

Conference on English Education (2009). *CEE position statement: Beliefs about social justice in English education.* First Biennial CEE Conference. Chicago: CEE. Retrieved from http://www.ncte.org/cee/positions/socialjustice.

Croce, K. (2018). Refugee students arrive at school: What happens next? *Global Education Review, 5*(4), 7–16.

Daniel, S. M. (2019). Writing our identities for successful endeavors: Resettled refugee youth look to the future. *Journal of Research in Childhood Education, 33*(1), 71–83.

Delgado, R., & Stefancic, J. (2000). Introduction. In R. Delgado & J. Stefancic (Eds.), *Critical race theory: The cutting edge* (2nd edition). Temple University Press.

Dryden-Peterson, S. (2016). Refugee education: The crossroads of globalization. *Educational Researcher, 45*(9), 473–82.

Gay, G., & Kirkland, K. (2003). Developing cultural critical consciousness and self-reflection in preservice teacher education. *Theory into practice, 42*(3), 181–87.

Gorski, P. C., & Swalwell, K. (2015). Equity literacy for all. *Educational Leadership, 72*(6), 34–40.

Gorski, P. C. & Dalton, K. (2020). Striving for critical reflection in multicultural and social justice teacher education: Introducing a typology of reflection approaches. *Journal of Teacher Education, 71*(3), 357–68.

Grant, C. A., & Sleeter, C. E. (2006). *Turning on learning: Five approaches for multicultural teaching plans for race, class, gender and disability* (4th edition). Jossey-Bass, An Imprint of Wiley.

Immigration Research Initiative. (2023, March 7). Refugee resettlement per capita: Which states do the most? https://immresearch.org/publications/refugee-resettlement-per-capita-which-states-do-the-most/.

Immigration Research Initiative. (2022, December 14). Refugee resettlement is still below its level before the Trump years. https://immresearch.org/publications/refugee-resettlement-is-still-below-its-level-before-the-trump-years/.

Kincheloe, J. L. (2008). *Critical pedagogy primer* (vol. 1). Peter Lang.

Krogstad, J. M. (2019, October 7). Key facts about refugees to the U.S. Pew Research Center. https://www.pewresearch.org/short-reads/2019/10/07/key-facts-about-refugees-to-the-u-s/.

Ladson-Billings, G. (2006). From the achievement gap to the education debt: Understanding achievement in U.S. schools. *Educational Researcher, 35*(7), 3–12.

McBrien, J. L. (2005). Educational needs and barriers for refugee students in the United States: A review of the literature. *Review of educational research, 75*(3), 329–64.

Mendenhall, M., & Bartlett, L. (2018). Academic and extracurricular support for refugee students in the US: Lessons learned. *Theory Into Practice, 57*(2), 109–18.

Mishler, E. G. (1990). Validation in inquiry-guided research: The role of exemplars in narrative studies. *Harvard Educational Review, 60,* 415–42.

Mosselson, J. (2006). Roots and routes: A reimagining of refugee identity construction and the implications for schooling. *Current Issues in Comparative Education, 29.* Retrieved from https://scholarworks.umass.edu/cie_faculty_pubs/29.

Mthethwa-Sommers, S. & Kisiara, O. (2015). Listening to students from refugee backgrounds: Lessons for education professionals. *PennGSE Perspectives on Urban Education, 12*(1). Retrieved from https://www.urbanedjournal.org/archive/volume-12-issue-1-spring-2015/listening-students-refugee-backgrounds-lessons-education-profe.

Priestley, M., Biesta, G. J. J., & Robinson, S. (2015). Teacher agency: What is it and why does it matter? In R. Kneyber & J. Evers (Eds.), *Flip the system: Changing education from the bottom up.* Routledge.

Sealey-Ruiz, Y. (2022). An archaeology of self for our times. *English Journal, 111*(5), 21–26.

Strekalova, S. & Hoot, J. L. (2008). What is special about special needs of refugee children?: Guidelines for teachers. *Multicultural Education, 16*(1), 21–24.

Strekalova-Hughes, E. (2019). Unpacking refugee flight: Critical content analysis of picturebooks featuring refugee protagonists. *International Journal of Multicultural Education, 21*(2), 23–44.

Strekalova-Hughes, E. & Nash, K. T. (2017, September). Toward a refugee critical race theory in early childhood education. Paper presented at the Annual Conference of the European Early Childhood Education Research Association, Bologna, Italy.

Swalwell, K. (2013). "With great power comes great responsibility": Privileged students' conceptions of justice-oriented citizenship. *Democracy & Education, 21*(1). Available at https://democracyeducationjournal.org/home/vol21/iss1/5.

Ukpodoku, O. N. (2007). Preparing socially conscious teachers: A social justice-oriented teacher education. *Multicultural Education, 15*(1), 8–15.

United Nations Office of the High Commission for Refugees. (2023). Figures at a glance. https://www.unhcr.org/us/about-unhcr/who-we-are/figures-glance#:~:text=How%20many%20refugees%20are%20there,are%20nearly%2032.5%20million%20refugees. Accessed June 13, 2023.

Vargas, S. R. (2003). Critical race theory in education: Theory, praxis, and recommendations. In G. R. López, & L. Parker (Eds.), *Interrogating racism in qualitative research methodology* (pp. 1–28). Peter Lang.
Wang, C., Strekalova-Hughes, E., & Cho, H. (2019). Going beyond a single story: Experiences and education of refugee children at home, in school, and in the community. *Journal of Research in Childhood Education, 33*(1), 1–5, DOI:10.1080/02568543.2018.1531670.

Chapter 2

Critical Consciousness and White Saviorism in Teacher Narratives

This chapter delves into the contradictory and complex ways that White teacher narratives demonstrate aspirations toward critical consciousness while also embodying aspects of White saviorism. It explores the narratives of two White suburban, midwestern public-high-school teachers. Chloe, an ESL teacher, and Jill, an ELA teacher, narrate their passionate convictions around their roles supporting refugee and displaced students. Both teachers demonstrate a keen sense of self-awareness and sociopolitical consciousness that can be leveraged in fostering teacher professional development toward critical consciousness-raising.

CRITICAL CONSCIOUSNESS

"Critical" means awareness of power and the processes and structures that hold it in place within any given context, like schooling. Critical educators ask questions of themselves and others about aspects of the educational domain, including, for example, social interactions, physical space and resources, technologies, texts, curricula, and even the nature of knowledge. They also recognize that classrooms exist as microcosms of the larger social, political, economic, and historic contexts surrounding them. Key questions critical educators ask include "Who has power in this situation? Who doesn't? What does power look like here?"

Critical consciousness names oppression and works to eradicate it. It calls educators to perceive unjust social power structures, investigate their causes, and visualize and enact alternatives and challenges to the status quo toward liberation from oppression for themselves and others (Gay & Kirkland, 2003). Within the politically contentious and rigid institutional structures of public schooling in the United States, critically conscious teachers are particularly vulnerable. This chapter examines several areas upon which teachers of refugee and displaced students might particularly focus their efforts.

The first is awareness and knowledge of their own and students' cultural capital (Bordieu, 1985). Cultural capital is the knowledge that is passively inherited by individuals within a sociocultural milieu. It consists of the symbols, ideas, tastes and preferences that group insiders can strategically deploy to access resources. For example, students who come to school as English dominant speakers have more cultural capital. Being born as a White English-speaker in the majority organically improves social outcomes, including educational outcomes, in US schools.

As the authors also discuss in Chapter 6, educators can also embrace notions of community cultural capital, or the knowledge, skills, abilities, and networks that students bring to school (Yosso, 2005). Schools that value and draw upon families' aspirational, linguistic, familial, social, navigational, and resistant capital are able to "transform education" by utilizing "assets that are already abundant" in students' and their families' communities (p. 82).

A closely related concept is meritocracy. Meritocracy is the ideology that anyone can get ahead if they work hard enough, regardless of social, political, or economic status. It is a meta-narrative that perpetuates racism. It is also a common trope of Whiteness that propels White saviorism. White saviors are those who reach down to lift up, or who provide access to the deserving few, so that they, too, can realize their merit.

Another important area in which teachers can develop critical consciousness is awareness and knowledge of the political nature of the English language and its relationship to US citizenship. English-only instruction is required in some states and an expectation in others. English is the entry point to academic and social growth within schools and communities. It carries with it, however, the oppressive weight of a colonial past and present. It is tied to naturalization, higher education and employment opportunities, and full membership in society.

WHITE SAVIORISM

White saviorism is a term used to critically describe the ways in which White people see themselves as liberating, rescuing, or uplifting non-White people. At the institutional level, it is a function of Whiteness known as the White savior industrial complex (WSIC). The WSIC is a "confluence of practices, processes, and institutions that reify historical inequities to ultimately validate White privilege" (Anderson, 2013, p. 39). Widely understood in the history of Western imperialism, White saviorism continues to show up centuries later within classroom walls across America through empathy, niceness, and generalizations.

It is widely recognized that, inspired by Hollywood's favorite films, wide audiences consume the romanticization of White women who save Black children from a cycle of poverty and failure (see, e.g., Aronson, 2017; Hughey, 2014). The death of American rapper Coolio resurfaced his most notable hit, "Gangsta's Paradise" (Coolio, 1995) in *Dangerous Minds* (Simpson, Bruckheimer, & Smith, 1995), which replayed the concept of White saviorism. Later, the theme appeared in movies like *Freedom Writers* (LaGravenese, 2007) and, most recently, *The Blind Side* (Hancock, 2009) and *The Help* (Taylor, 2011).

In teachers' stories, the vacillation between conscious recognition of Whiteness and dysconscious racism (King, 1991) draws attention. King defines dysconscious racism as "limited and distorted understandings . . . about inequity and cultural diversity—understandings that make it difficult . . . to act in favor of truly equitable education" (p. 134). For example, one meta-narrative about public education is that it is a free and accessible system for all and, perhaps, what is assumed to be the most equitable institution available to youth in the United States. Dysconscious racism, however, is responsible for the persistence of inequitable opportunities and outcomes.

In the following sections, the authors examine how Chloe and Jill narrate themselves as striving toward critical consciousness within schools permeated by Whiteness and White saviorism. Through Chloe's found poem (see box 2.1), the authors portray Chloe as a teacher who is critically aware of her own intersectional identities. She negotiates the difference between her Whiteness, privilege, and educational influence in search of the best way to maximize student potential and increase her connection with displaced learners.

Also understanding that their background information of education is going to be different and that truly to have social justice within the classroom, you have to be aware of those cultural backgrounds and those religious backgrounds and even their personal backgrounds.

CHLOE'S STORY

Chloe describes herself as a White, South African, American, Muslim woman. She communicates, bringing her whole self to the conversation, that White teachers' identities are not always easily categorized. Chloe stamps her identity, expressing "I am White, my skin is White, I'm American . . . [and], overall I'm very American." She uses her "jumbled" and "complex cultural identity" as a point of reference in working with her displaced learners.

Chloe

My identity is very complex, because I am White, my skin is White, I'm American./It's hard for me to pick apart what parts of me make me South African/I think overall I'm very American./They see me as kind of a foreigner because of my perspectives./So it's kind of in this limbo of what I am./Even though my complex cultural identity is kind of jumbled. /But . . . you're White./And sometimes I've noticed it kind of makes me a little defensive . . . that I have to prove myself as a Muslim woman even though I know it shouldn't matter. Right?//

When you're dealing with a refugee family and students, already they're kind of at a disadvantage, right? Them coming here, a lot of times it wasn't their choice, right?/They're kind of used as the crutch, right?//I think when it comes to education, as a teacher, I have more of a duty or obligation to make sure that the students that I'm teaching that, I mean all students should have meaningful work, but that their work is even more meaningful.//

At the time of the interview, Chloe was in her second year of teaching students that she described as Black, East African, and Muslim in a suburban, midwestern public high school. She notes a disjunction between her racial and religious identities when she declares, I am "a White woman who is Muslim. I wear [a] hijab or turban." Furthermore, Chloe's social and professional identity is complicated due to the friction between her religion and race, centering race as the main barrier that makes it "harder to connect because automatically there's kind of, I feel like there's a wall there."

CRITICAL CONSCIOUSNESS IN CHLOE'S NARRATIVES

Chloe's overlapping identities create multiple lenses and a unique perspective on social justice. She is clearly cognizant of the tensions between race and lived experiences. When this is disrupted by her visible Whiteness (she recollects her students' input on her Whiteness, "But . . . you're White"), it is followed with a great sense of awareness. She declares, "And sometimes I've noticed it kind of makes me a little defensive." Noticing and naming this defensiveness is an important step in developing critical consciousness.

Her Islamic background, uninterrupted by her Whiteness during Ramadan and Eid, allow her to recognize the misinterpretation of equity and equality:

I have a colleague who says, "Oh I want to be head of the equity team because I think everyone should be equal and be given the same chance." All the while she was willing to put on a prom during Ramadan. And not understand the concept of how our Eid goes by the moon, not just by a calendar. And getting very upset that now she can't plan because maybe Eid will be a different day.

Chloe unravels the macro-aggression of routine, specifically in the scheduling of prom during a religious obligation for her Muslim displaced students. It is significant that the macro-aggression is embodied in the character of an equity-inspired colleague, a potential leader of the school's equity team. At the same time, Chloe's unproblematic acceptance of "prom" is a distinct reminder of the cultural capital passed down as a way of honoring the social and cultural expectations of those in power. The focus on prom's timing, rather than its origins, purpose, and meanings dysconsciously shifts attention as has been found in other teacher narratives (Cross, Behizadeh, & Holihan, 2018).

In this way, Chloe challenges the status quo but leaves institutional traditions in place with inadvertent consequences. Her inclusion of "very" in describing her American identity provides a holistic view of the notion of cultural capital, implying not only the economic understanding of the word but also an immaterial understanding in relation to her role as an expert in the English language and the American culture. She says, "Education is everything. There is this connotation of, 'Oh, they're coming to the United States and they can't even speak English.'"

Unlike her displaced learners, Chloe holds cultural capital—familiarity with the legitimate culture within a society. As a result, Chloe channels her intrinsic understanding of American culture and English education, particularly the spoken and unspoken resistance to displaced learners, because they need additional resources to fit into American attitudes, values, and norms and better benefit the American education system.

Like Chloe, many teachers struggle to mobilize their own and their displaced learners' capital in terms of power, agency, and influence. In the United States, people in general are impatient with both teachers and displaced learners. Language learners continue to be tested more than any other group, and teachers continue to be publicly scrutinized and measured more than any other profession. For Chloe, joint efforts boil down to activism and equity. She says, "I think activism and equity should go hand in hand."

WHITE SAVIORISM IN CHLOE'S NARRATIVES

Throughout Chloe's inquiry response emerges a narrative based on "difficult life transitions and trauma" (Reissman, 1993, p. 4). Three years into her teaching career, Chloe spotlights jargon associated with the group of learners she supports, demonstrating knowledge and awareness, "A SLIFE is a student with interrupted periods of learning." Young in her career, Chloe searches to articulate her level of expertise in the education of displaced learners, "I know with families, so some of our students, their parents don't speak English . . . but it can be difficult for the students because they're kind of used as the crutch, right?"

Chloe's use of "crutch" as a metaphor for how students broker language for their families is significant. In this way, Chloe presents how, in an attempt to support displaced learners' English-language acquisition, teachers internalize language barriers as an over-encompassing deficit that impacts home and school life. They also refuse to acknowledge their students' community cultural capital (Yosso, 2005).

The deficit lens perpetuates White saviorism among well-intentioned teachers who witness the struggle of learning a second language among displaced learners. Teachers often dysconsiously transfer that struggle to other aspects of learners' life, as illustrated in Chloe's statement, "That gives us [teachers] insight to our students. Insight into what they're dealing with at home and how maybe our approaches and how we can build relationships will be very different from other students."

When Chloe calls on teachers to build relationships with refugee and displaced students that will be "very different from other students," she balances intuition with intellect. Her end goal is to create a sense of agency and autonomy. She says, "I have more of a duty or obligation to make sure . . . that their [displaced learners'] work is even more meaningful." She sheds light on an open-minded effort to develop "meaningful" educational opportunities for displaced learners, meaning more student-centered and responsive to the student rather than the narrative that shadows them.

Chloe's effort is complicated by the complexity of White saviorism, which protrudes out of a place of great awareness of one's own privilege, particularly in relationship to refugee students. She notes that they are "already at a mind of disadvantage, right? Because they were torn from their home . . . it wasn't their choice, right?" Chloe's internal acknowledgment of her "duty and obligation" as a teacher of displaced learners, which aligns with the overall social identity of a teacher, entangles with the global imagery of refugee students—a story about pain, injury, and healing.

Chloe further discusses the disadvantages that lead to cultural conflicts, demonstrating an awareness of imminent tensions that inadvertently chip at relationship-building when it comes to displaced learners:

> Right? If you have a student that just came from a camp that had maybe little to no plumbing, no infrastructure or no type of education, coming to a school, knowing the routine is going to be weird for them and it's going to take time. Understanding the student-teacher relationship. You can't expect a student to say please and thank you and raise their hand when they talk right away. Or even to have maybe some, not politeness, but the social etiquettes that we in the United States value.

No doubt clashes in cultural values and language barriers delay the relationship between teachers and displaced language learners. This delay ultimately comes with a cost in achievement and social growth and development. Chloe's social and educational awareness of identities is personal. Young and inexperienced in the high-school classroom, Chloe witnesses short-term struggles that will fester into long-term social struggles for a group of students who are closer to her than to her teacher colleagues in age, religion, and continent of origin.

Like Chloe, Jill anticipates the struggle of displaced students and projects a keen sense of awareness of identity, culture, standards for success, and equity. Unlike Chloe, Jill brings over twenty years of teaching experience. Jill shares lessons learned on students' intrinsic motivation and students' capability to perform because, after all, Jill explains, "I was that kid." See box 2.2 for a found poem about Jill.

JILL'S STORY

This portrait of Jill focuses on her strong sense of individualism. Her experience as a "widowed single mom" has been like being alone "on an island." She stands out because she majored in both English and biology ("a weird combo"), is not religiously conservative like the community in which she landed her first teaching job, and is an "open-minded artist" who "thinks for [herself]" due to her family's influence.

Jill is a determined and committed mother and teacher, solidly invested in supporting her son and her students in similar ways—they are all "her kids." Her passionate convictions and belief in her students are inspiring. She says that she understands the financial burdens faced by students who rely on scholarships to attend college in the United States. She recognizes that she has racial and linguistic advantages, or community cultural capital (Yosso,

Jill

I went to [a college] now a university,/And I majored in biology and English—/A weird combo./I think that's why I like grammar . . . it's structured.//I've been teaching in the same school/In the same room/For twenty-one years.//Super organized.//I first taught in a really,/really, /really/Conservative community./(Really conservative.)/It seemed so strange to me.//I was the outsider—/I bring an open-mindedness./I love having the insight of those kids in my class,/My kids—/The kids of all different backgrounds./I love hearing that./Conscious/of what I know/ And what I don't know./If I don't know, I need to ask—/Fine line.//

My parents are artists./They raised us to think for ourselves./We did not have money at all./I was that kid./So I get it,/I get it.//We all believe in the rights of people, and that everyone should have rights./I'm a White woman in Minnesota, which in itself is an advantage./I believe you make your own opportunities./I don't care where you came from,/I don't care where you're going./But my belief is in you now./There's something good in you, and we're going to find it.//I [am] a widowed single mom,/I see things sort of differently, too./Being a single widowed mom is an island on your own, for sure./I've never really met anyone else like me./It's me. It falls on me.

2005), alongside her students, and she firmly advocates and holds high expectations for them.

Jill studied education at a midwestern liberal-arts college. She chose secondary education in addition to her dual majors (English and biology) during her junior year. She completed her first seven years of teaching in the same town as the college. She felt out of place there, given the close-knit community and the "conservative" culture of the school and its "lack of diversity," which she describes as "a little bubble." After seven years, she moved to the suburban city where she now teaches.

She explains that, in her time at her current high school, she has taught all of the English classes offered to ninth to twelfth graders, including honors, literature and novel courses, and professional writing for English learners and special-education students. At the time of the interview, eighty-five percent of the students in her professional-writing course were English learners.

Jill has earned veteran teacher status at her school; in fact, she can almost be bestowed the title of historian. Jill depicts learning and teaching as being more of a craft than an art. She values consistency, structure, and organization. She says, "I think that's why I like grammar . . . it's structured." In writing, the focus on grammatical styling choices to ensure clarity and messaging demands more craft than art. The focus on grammar reinforces Jill's narrative involving doing things skillfully by hand, intentionally and thoughtfully.

CRITICAL CONSCIOUSNESS IN JILL'S NARRATIVES

Jill holds high expectations for her students. She talks about "her belief in them." Her perspective is asset-based because she talks more about what her students bring to their learning than what they lack. She reports that, over the years, her honors classes, considered "pre-AP," and her speech classes began to fill with English learners (ELs) with refugee backgrounds. Jill describes her feelings in the following way:

> So to me, I just love it. I love it. Every time I see a new EL kid who ends up taking honors, I'm like, "Yes!" I have more Somali and refugee students in my honors classes now than I've ever had in the past, which has been so wonderful. And I would only assume that it's going to grow. But to get them excited, to be involved and feel some ownership of their world here is great. So I talked these two girls into being in speech and they ended up advancing to the state. It was amazing. The whole room was just, it was so powerful. You just have to ask, "What is your strength? What is your niche?"

In this way, Jill aspires toward an identity as a culturally relevant teacher—that is, one who persistently holds high expectations. Such beliefs are important for Jill's work as an advocate for her students. Jill also aspires to be critically conscious of the literature that is the focus of instruction in her literature-survey classes. She searches for literature that resonates with her students' experiences but also matches their reading levels and their English-language abilities.

Like any skilled teacher, Jill understands the connection between fluency, motivation, reading ability, and linguistic repertoire. She feels that, by doing this, she is "giving kids a better shot." When her high-school–aged students perform below grade level on reading, she says, "They just may not know about sentence structure. What we offer for reading—I want to find fourth grade [leveled] books that are not immature. I don't want them to feel stupid, because they're not stupid."

Alongside her department colleagues, Jill critically examines texts and curriculum to ensure that "all voices are heard." Culturally relevant text selection is, of course, important in every classroom. Teachers of refugee and displaced students, however, often struggle to find resources. Jill positions herself and her colleagues as aspiring toward critical consciousness when she says, "So I think we, as a language arts department, have really worked hard to make sure that all voices are heard, especially even in the resources that we use, we want to make sure that kids feel that they're represented."

Critically conscious educators of refugee and displaced students also have a keen awareness and knowledge of the political processes that place students in their classrooms and their educational rights. Awareness of ideologies of citizenship, what it means to be American, and civil rights come to the forefront in Jill's pedagogical choices:

> Whenever I hear just social justice in itself, I always go back to the rights that you have, and that all kids in a room feel like they have that same opportunity, and that they see themselves respected in whatever I do, whether it be a writing assignment or a reading assignment. That to me is hugely important.

Critical pedagogues debate the value of schooling and argue that the meritocracy myth holds this value in place. The authors, however, believe that Jill, with her "no-nonsense" approach to promoting educational rights, aspires toward a critical consciousness reminiscent of liberation pedagogy. She "see[s] the value of an education as being something freeing" and she wants her students to "see that." She adds, "I hope that I can help them find ways to get those opportunities and to realize them."

Jill is conscious of the ways that school structures oppress students identified with special needs, especially during times of crisis like the COVID-19 pandemic. She reports that protocols for distance learning necessitated an inequitable conflation of English-learner and special-education learner needs. For the first time in twenty years, her professional-writing course was filled with both kinds of students. On the one hand, according to Jill, the arrangement worked well because there were three co-teachers to manage the in-class, online, and hybrid format.

On the other hand, as Jill describes the situation to her interviewer, she adds, "Yeah, I know." To the authors, Jill seemed to be showing her awareness of her own vulnerability alongside her concern for her students' situation. While Jill doesn't explicitly challenge it, she certainly perceives it:

> And that's what teaching is. You need to be there. You need to be present. So there's three of us in that room at the same time. And what we've been doing is we're kind of rotating through what we're doing. We're trying to move on, but we're really gauging it by the kids. And the nice thing is that having three of us, when I'm teaching, one of the other teachers is manning the Google Meet and answering questions that come up on the chat. And then the third teacher is walking around addressing any specific questions. And usually, the EL teacher is the one who's walking around, because the vast majority of that class is EL.

Another way in which Jill aspires toward critical consciousness is in the ways that she talks about change. She believes that "if you believe there needs to be change, then you need to be one of the people who makes the change." She describes herself as "the one that will jump in front of the bully" and says that she doesn't "have a lot of fear." She advises her students "if you lose friends, then you have to question the friends you're losing. And maybe they weren't good friends to begin with."

Further, she addresses the need for changing the systems that limit access and opportunities. She calls for increased collaboration between guidance counselors and classroom teachers who do not often encourage English learners to take classes in, for example, the honors program. She worries that kids "shy away from honors classes when they don't have friends in [the classes]." She adds, "I hope we [the city] evolve more, because these kids have so much to offer. And when there's these people that don't want to hear what they have to offer, I think it's sad. You lose out on some amazing kids when you put up that wall. I just hate it. It makes me sad."

As she aspires toward critical consciousness, Jill also calls upon the school district to do more in terms of professional development:

> I just wish the district would do more to educate us. I feel like it's great that the students are helping us learn more about them, but certainly the district could do more. I have learned more about Somali culture from my students than I ever did from any in-service. I always felt they just weren't hitting what we needed to know.

WHITE SAVIORISM IN JILL'S NARRATIVES

In an effort to show solidarity with her displaced learners, Jill tells a story of being "that kid," addressing her own financial insecurities. She says, "We did not have money at all," followed by "So, I get it, I get it." Jill spotlights the global imagery of refugee students and aspires to single-handedly construct space for growth from the loss and the financial insecurities of the past in an effort to take hold of the future. She adds, "There's something good in you, and we're going to find it. It's me. It falls on me."

As Jill aspires toward critical consciousness, the authors see the shadow of White saviorism undergirding Jill's belief in students. By noting the goodness there is to locate in learners, she implies a need or an absence of such. Like Chloe, a sense of obligation to relate to and to support displaced learners "differently" shows up in Jill's narratives.

Jill describes herself as a "super organized . . . outsider . . . conscious . . . [with an] open-mindedness."

Her story, though, is also blindsided by White saviorism, which shows up in the separation between Jill and "those kids." To tread with focus and clarity, the subtle use of "those kids" throughout the narratives is not racism or discrimination but displays a stark separation that insinuates a barrier or a disconnection in the educational transaction between displaced learners and their teachers:

> I would say their [refugee and displaced students'] greatest strength would be that huge desire to achieve. Those kids really, really want to learn. They see what can happen with an education and they want that. And so I love that they have that drive. I feel in general, their parents are very supportive of them. It is a language barrier. They are smart kids who simply don't know the language. And if you pick one of our American kids up and throw them into Italy and say, okay, go there. Are they going to come off as not knowing what they're talking about or not understanding? So I feel like we have a huge gap with these kids that are being treated like they are just not smart. And it has nothing to do with intelligence and everything to do with language.

Jill acknowledges displaced learners' eagerness to learn, learning independence, flexibility, and organization. The use of "they [displaced learners]" versus "our American" highlights the startling underlying discomfort in cognitive dissonance among teachers supporting displaced learners. Jill presents a tension and anxiety in which she balances her preconceived notions against the reality of her time period.

Jill's years of experience foster her desire to center content, actual teaching, over the background and realities of her displaced learners. She says, "I don't care where you came from. I don't care where you're going." By primarily focusing on the teaching of grammar, structure, and the potential "possibilities," Jill avoids divisive topics related to "those kids" in regard to race and additional barriers.

She dodges topics some consider anachronistic, unnecessary, and trouble-making, at the same time acknowledging a clear moral compass. She says, "We all believe in the rights of people, and that everyone should have rights." Jill's statements about the "rights of all people" and that "you make your own opportunities" can also be seen as the meritocracy myth in action.

Despite a shift in student population, Jill teaches grammar, constitutive of Western capital, to imbue a structural tone in the classroom space and student learning. This tone inadvertently makes learning opportunities more accessible to those who inherit White language from their White American culture, excluding displaced learners foreign to the culture of Standard American English.

Worse, as argued by Bonilla-Silva (2012), "[R]acial domination necessitates something like a grammar to normalize the standards of white supremacy as the standard for all sorts of everyday transactions rendering domination almost invisible" (p. X). The focus here is not to call on teachers to stop teaching grammar; that would be an oxymoron coming from a language arts teacher. The authors, however, aim to prompt a reflection on how a teacher's personal preference for teaching English language structure (grammar) to the exclusion of its social, historical, and political meanings creates additional barriers to learning and, perhaps, an unwelcoming tone.

REFLECTION

The authors especially invite educators serving refugee and displaced learners to reflect on how being an educator in the United States creates complexities that trigger insecurities around ensuring academic readiness while also providing equitable access and opportunities for displaced students. The chapter seeks to interrupt White saviorism and its accompanying internalized White guilt in order to unpack tensions that are inherently present, to some extent, in the narratives of all White teachers in the United States.

As noted in the Introduction, the authors offer this discussion first to devote space for reflection and growth. The chapter resists popular false assumptions of White saviorism, especially the overdone tropes that perpetuate racial and social harm on displaced students. Using Chloe and Jill's insightful responses, the chapter asserts, that like everything in life, there's a positive light that occasionally beams through the darkness of White saviorism, especially when infused with personal awareness and an invitation for more perspective.

Chloe and Jill are intrinsically motivated to create welcoming spaces and opportunities for success for their displaced learners; however, those intentions are often interrupted and disrupted by a politically charged landscape that scrutinizes the outcomes of teachers and refugees. Although this chapter appears to jump on board with the scrutiny of society, it's important to recall that narrative analysis happens in collaboration. Analysis of these narratives brings to the surface how authenticity is often complicated by social context, creating an active struggle between conscious and subconscious—what one knows versus what one thinks one knows.

An important question for educators to consider is the following: "How does a teacher's personal experience, personal needs, and personal goals to 'make a difference' show up in the classroom space?" Employing the lenses of Whiteness and White saviorism to better understand teachers' stories can help to unpack their nuances.

The nuances of success in a capitalistic society create additional burdens for teachers and displaced learners. The lack of clarity around words like academic success, belonging, and achievement sustains learning environments that inherit assumptions rooted in the lived experiences of White teachers. Teachers who predominantly do not mirror their classroom audience face complexities of White saviorism.

When it comes to displaced learners, Chloe and Jill's adopted narrative aligns with the global thirty-second commercial of "for just one dollar a day, you can save a life." Chloe compares her learners to "crutches." Jill creates a distinct separation between herself and her students when she calls them "those kids." Both teachers believe it is their call and obligation to save displaced learners from a socioeconomic abyss.

At the same time, both teachers aspire toward a critical consciousness that values questioning and self-reflection. Jill says, "You have to be ok with not knowing. When in doubt, just ask a question." She acknowledges that "sometimes questions can be uncomfortable." Jill remains "conscious of what [she] knows and what [she doesn't] know." She is unafraid to ask questions and walk that "fine line."

REFERENCES

Anderson, A. (2013). Teacher for America and the dangers of deficit thinking. *CriticalEducation, 4(11), 28–47.*

Aronson, B. (2017). The White savior industrial complex: A cultural studies analysis of a teacher educator, savior film, and future teachers. *Journal of Critical Thought and Praxis, 6*(3), 36–54.

Bonilla-Silva, E. (2012). The invisible weight of whiteness: The racial grammar of everyday life in contemporary America. *Ethnic and racial studies, 35*(2), 173–94.

Bourdieu, P. (1985). The forms of capital. In J. Richardson (Ed.), *Handbook of theory and research for the sociology of education.* Greenwood.

Coolio (1995). *Gangsta's paradise.* Tommy Boy.

Cross, S. B., Behizadeh, N., & Holihan, J. (2018). Critically conscious or dangerouslydysconscious?: An analysis of teacher candidates' concerns in urban schools. *The Teacher Educator*, 53:2, 124–49. doi: 10.1080/08878730.2017.1416212.

Gay, G., & Kirkland, K. (2003). Developing cultural critical consciousness and self-reflection in preservice teacher education. *Theory Into Practice, 42*(3), 181–87.

Hancock, J. L. (2009). *The Blind Side.* Warner Brothers.

Hughey, M. W. (2014). The white savior film: Content, critics, and consumption. Temple University Press.

King, J. (1991). Dysconscious racism: Ideology, identity, and the miseducation of teachers. *Journal of Negro Education, 60*(2), 133–46. doi:10.2307/2295605.

LaGravenese, R. (2007). *Freedom Writers.* Paramount Pictures.

Reissman, C. K. (1993). *Narrative analysis.* Sage Publications, Inc.
Simpson, D., Bruckheimer, J., & Smith, J. N. (1995). *Dangerous minds*. Buena Vista Pictures.
Taylor, T. (2011). *The Help*. Walt Disney Studios Motion Pictures.
Yosso, T. J. (2005). Whose culture has capital? A critical race theory discussion of community cultural wealth. *Race, Ethnicity, and Education, 8*(1), 69–91.

Chapter 3

Changemaking and Resisting

In this chapter, the authors narrate the experiences of two educators, Elizabeth and Kaylee, who both talk about themselves as changemakers and resisters. Their classrooms are in a suburban, midwestern high school. They teach in a new-to-country program that is part of a school-within-a-school model, where students begin their education journey in the United States. This chapter focuses on the ways that Elizabeth and Kaylee narrate the practices and perspectives that create a welcoming learning space for newcomer learners.

EDUCATORS AS CHANGEMAKERS

Changemakers is a popular term, originally stemming from the work of Bill Drayton and the Ashoka Organization. It was conceived to define the qualities of social entrepreneurs. This chapter builds upon the term to emphasize the ways that Elizabeth and Kaylee establish themselves as pedagogical entrepreneurs. Dal, Elo, Leffler, Svedberg, and Westerberg (2016) define pedagogical entrepreneurship as "a[n] approach connected to the human qualities and skills that make it possible for individuals within organizations and communities to act flexibly and creatively when meeting rapid social and economic changes" (p. 161).

As pedagogical entrepreneurs, Elizabeth and Kaylee perpetually seek improvement through change. They value agency, empathy, and advocacy for their students (McInerney, 2020). Some existing ideas of changemakers in education describe how teachers might encourage and support their students in developing autonomy, agency, and advocacy skills (Burridge & Buchanan, 2022; Jacobs, Chau, & Hamzah, 2022; McInerney, 2020). However, Elizabeth and Kaylee extend this notion of changemaker—they focus on changing the system rather than changing the student to better fit the system. While both are important, this chapter argues that teachers can, and should, embrace the role of changemakers themselves.

By imagining alternative approaches that may better adapt to the changing needs of students, Elizabeth and Kaylee speak of creating opportunities for learners to connect to each other in "non-traditional learning spaces" where they can learn cooperatively in a "creative atmosphere" (Dal et al, 2016, p. 173). The nontraditional classrooms in which they work are, by their very structure, creative atmospheres. They are uniquely designed for newly arrived refugee and displaced students. They are creative atmospheres not only because they differ from the traditional school-within-a-school model, but because of pedagogical entrepreneurs, like Elizabeth and Kaylee, who resist traditional models that are unfit for refugee and displaced students.

RESISTANCE

Resistance might be envisioned as a refusal to accept or comply with something or to prevent something by action or argument. It can be defined as the ability to not be affected by something. Scholars have written about how teachers of refugee students can offer "pockets of resistance," which act as models of social justice (McKeon, Merchant, Flanagan-Gonzalas, & Sultan, 2022, p. 8). The impacts of educators' localized resistance can influence the context in which they work and "create safe spaces where refugee children thrive" (p. 6). In order to better understand the nuanced ways that Kaylee and Elizabeth resist, the authors adopted the idea of resistance as a force that slows, refuses, or negates the effect of another force.

Social-justice–oriented educators can resist social order, slow pressures, and counter the status quo in order to better support newcomer refugee and displaced students. Elizabeth and Kaylee resist through critically viewing norms and offering alternatives. They respond to and negate assumptions about their students. In the stories that follow, for example, Elizabeth identifies and rejects privilege, power, and authority in herself (McKeon et al., 2022, p. 17). Kaylee "disperse[s]" power and "challenges the prevailing discourse" (p. 18). Next, the authors offer portraits of Elizabeth and Kaylee as gleaned through conversational interviews. See box 3.1 for Elizabeth's found poem.

ELIZABETH'S STORY

Elizabeth seeks to understand herself and how her identity affects relationships with others, especially her students. She notices how her identity is co-constructed. Elizabeth realizes that how she self-identifies may or may not align with others'—especially her students'—perceptions of her. She believes

Elizabeth

A native English speaker, monolingual,/middle-class, White/nearing forty-year-old woman,/mother and wife/born, and I have lived my whole life in central [name of state].//Age, language, gender, race—/ really meaningful in my students' perception of me/from the first time students meet me.//It's not as important for me/because it's easy to ignore since I am the/dominant race in the room,/but I'm sure it's significant to my students.//Teaching fifteen years/English, but also other subjects as an EL teacher/Only teaching English-language learners/ From the start of my career, I was primarily teaching refugee students.//

Started teaching when there was a large influx of refugees settling// Largely from East Africa, mostly Somali-speaking,/some Vietnamese students,/some Central American or Mexican students//Communicating in a language that is neither their first or my first//Undergraduate in anthropology/It's the perfect background for what I do/But I think the more valuable role it's played/is in my willingness to see my own culture./And I think that that's not something that a lot of people are unwilling to do,/it's just really hard./Helps me reflect really personally on my own bias and my own assumptions/what my culture is bringing to my perception of things

Helps me talk to students who I know might have different cultural experience/Helps me to not be judgmental or make assumptions/how other people see the world around them.//Strong advocate for my English learners/It's part of my identity in terms of the career I chose./I chose a career where I would be feeling as though/I'm helping people. Making a difference./It's so much a part of my identity and a part of my life.//

her age, gender, and race are important because they influence this positioning. Her students' perceptions are informed by the social meanings of age, gender, and race in this classroom, in the communities outside of this classroom, and in the communities from which students come. The communities from which Elizabeth's students arrive are ever present. Elizabeth embraces nuanced understandings of her own identity and those of her students.

A significant part of Elizabeth's found poem reflects how she chooses a role of inquiry and investment. She notes that her anthropology background supports her in resisting the biases or generalizations that may influence her work and her students' interactions with her if she were instead passive. It is important that she chooses this career and this active role because her work in this role is intentional.

Elizabeth describes herself as a middle-class, White woman, mother, and wife. She is a monolingual native speaker of English. She was born and has lived in the same geographic area in which she currently teaches. She is nearing forty years old. At the time of the interviews, Elizabeth was an educator at this public high school for fifteen years, teaching English and a variety of content subjects to multilingual students learning English. During her career, the term "new to country" has shifted but continues to signify an evolving demographic with the same purpose—to give these students their first exposure to English and the US school system. Elizabeth continues to work in the same building as a language specialist, supporting new-to-country students.

She earned a bachelor's degree in anthropology and a master's degree in teaching English as a second language (TESL), which included licensure for K–12 ESL teaching. She emphasizes how her interest in cultural anthropology helps her view the biases and assumptions she holds, which affect how she views her students and her work. Specifically, her background in anthropology helps her to view her own culture, which helps her better understand the influences that cause her to view herself and others in certain ways.

According to Elizabeth, her career began at the same time as an influx of refugees settled into the city and school where she taught. She reports that decades before the start of her career, when Elizabeth grew up in the area, it was largely "White, Christian, and homogeneous." The city has continued to be home to newly displaced and refugee families throughout her career.

ELIZABETH AS A CHANGEMAKER

Elizabeth narrates herself as a changemaker, especially in the ways she shares alternative ideas with colleagues and works to increase their awareness of biases. She describes a team meeting when she was enthusiastic about her team's earnest engagement in one particular conversation about assessment. Elizabeth had been collaborating with this team of teachers, in the role of language specialist and co-teacher, for over three years. At the time of the conversation, the COVID-19 pandemic had accelerated the need for innovation and entrepreneurship.

Elizabeth and her team struggled with challenges of online learning. For example, a typical assessment might be an in-class, proctored exam. During the shift to distance learning, the team had been, in Elizabeth's words, "working really hard to write assessments differently." Elizabeth recalls that teammates raised language-specific observations. She reports that they made statements like, "Well, that type of question might be difficult to understand for some students who have limited English." They asked questions like,

"Well, if a kid's English is limited, won't it be difficult for them to respond verbally to questions?"

The team offered feedback about the linguistic bias of the assessment Elizabeth shared. In Elizabeth's narrative, this conversation represents a reversal of the typical roles they hold in a meeting like this. Elizabeth has worked in this role for many years in order to support students and build capacity in her colleagues. She joins meetings to offer her unique lens on students' identities and language development. Given these experiences as a language specialist co-teaching with content teachers, she recognizes this conversation as pivotal. She celebrates this shift in roles and what she perceives as a change in perspectives in her colleagues.

Her role is "transformed" when an educator, whose core focus is not language, demonstrates proficiency in asking critical questions about language bias. Elizabeth shares, "Three years ago I never would've imagined that in that room I wouldn't be the one asking those questions. I was just so happy." Elizabeth celebrates that her ability to act flexibly and think creatively about supporting newcomer refugees in content areas has enabled other educators to join her in changemaking that supports her students beyond her own classroom.

While changemakers may need to engage in small steps, like creating a single alternative assignment, or joining a meeting as a single, alternative voice, these small changes can be the building blocks for larger, systemic change (Jacobs et al., 2022). In that moment of reflection, Elizabeth identifies how work and collaboration with her colleagues over three years has spurred change in other educators' way of viewing refugee students. She describes the joy she experiences in drawing more educators into conversations about multilingualism and shifting educators to explore new mindsets.

The teachers demonstrated a shift in mindset when they adapted the linguistic lens that Elizabeth had modeled. The authors see that Elizabeth's work as a changemaker actualized in changing the thoughts and actions of her colleagues in a way that positively impacts refugee and displaced students. Elizabeth exhibits how being a changemaker equips her and her co-teacher to explore alternative assessment models made necessary by the new and changing demands on educators caused by the pandemic. Elizabeth experiences agency due to her collaborative work. Moreover, she witnesses the agency her partnerships and idea-sharing brings to other educators. The ripple effect of her work with this team grows changemakers.

Elizabeth's ability to adapt and innovate inspires her colleagues to ask critical questions and consider new lenses through which to view their work and students. In this way, her pedagogical entrepreneurship shifts responsibility for change from students to teachers. This is an important approach that extends the idea that teachers ought to develop students as changemakers (Burridge

& Buchanan, 2022; Jacobs, et al. 2022; McInerney, 2020). Elizabeth flips the responsibility not only to teachers but also from ESL teachers to all teachers.

ELIZABETH AS A RESISTER

As discussed, one form of resistance is to become a force that slows, refuses, or negates the effect of another force. In one narrative, Elizabeth responds to and negates negative assumptions about her students, namely, that if they are unsuccessful, it is because they choose not to take advantage of the "free education" offered to them. Elizabeth was in conversation with a colleague in her building, expressing her frustration with feeling ineffective in her teaching practice over the last few weeks.

Elizabeth remembers the colleague responding, intending to console her, with a reminder that all they could "offer" was "a free education." The teachers do their best with the resources they have, and they "shouldn't expect that much more or complain about what they can offer."-However, Elizabeth was far from consoled. She remembers leaving the conversation "just feeling gross" and "feeling really icky." In recounting this conversation, she refuses the colleague's devaluation of the free education Elizabeth offers. She says, "I don't care if it's a free education or a million dollar education, I'm still working as hard as I can possibly work to provide the best experience for the kids."

While Elizabeth acknowledges her feelings of frustration and ineffectiveness, she also recounts how she refuses to accept the systemic limitations her colleague describes. Though her position as a public educator is widely perceived as a piece of a failing or subpar system, she resists that role and image, for the sake of her students. Elizabeth describes how she works "as hard as [she] can possibly work" in order to emphasize her complete commitment to pushing up against challenges. Elizabeth positions herself as a changemaker when she describes her willingness to work against the weight of the system and the challenges under which she operates.

Elizabeth also acknowledges and examines Whiteness and how power and authority operate in her classroom. In the following narrative excerpt, she identifies and rejects privilege, power, and authority in herself:

> That's always an interesting conversation. And you've probably had it too, with really well-meaning thoughtful people [who] would say something like, "Well, you know what it's like to be the minority, you're the only White person in your classroom all the time." And you have to be like, "No, that is not what it means to be a minority." I may be the only White person in the classroom, but I am by far the most authoritarian. I have all the power. It's not the same.

She acknowledges the differences between her experiences as a White woman and those of her students as racialized minorities. She investigates and resists the normative roles associated with these externally imposed identities as a means of pushing toward a liminal space. In this in-between space, Elizabeth pushes back in conversations with her colleagues. She hopes that, even if power cannot be shifted completely by individual attitudes and interactions, at least she can interrupt it.

According to Elizabeth, this exchange is representative of a recurring conversation into which she is often drawn. She even suggests that the interviewer, who shares many of the same social identities as Elizabeth and identifies as White, has probably had this kind of conversation, too. The emphasis of the recurrence and generality of this conversation suggests that Elizabeth acknowledges how Whiteness permeates school spaces and how racism is perpetuated without explicit acts of racism.

When such conversations play themselves out repeatedly in different contexts, they are considered meta-narratives. Meta-narratives are the "grand narratives" that "function to legitimize power, authority, and social customs" (Lyotard, 1984). They shape beliefs that are taken as universal truths about socialized identities (like race) and embedded in deeply, often unexamined, ideologies which play out in conversations like those Elizabeth reports.

Elizabeth narrates her role and reply in this recurring conversation at the same time that she includes others in this outline of a general conversation. She frames a resistant response she and others may employ: "You have to be like, 'No, that is not what it means to be a minority.'" Elizabeth casts "you" in her narrative to represent herself, the listener, and other White teachers in this circumstance. Then, Elizabeth shifts back to personal pronouns when she reflects about her personal identity: "I may be the only White person in the classroom, but I am by far the most authoritarian. I have all the power. It's not the same."

Elizabeth positions herself as knowledgeable about her own privilege, power, and authority. She recognizes how her perspective is resistance to the nameless other participant in the conversation she describes. Elizabeth's knowledge and awareness is a juxtaposition to the ambiguous other person in the conversation, who represents a falsehood that is perpetuated by a broader societal norm. In this narrative, Elizabeth demonstrates how her understanding of race and power equips her to resist structures and falsehoods that may disadvantage or misrepresent refugee and displaced students.

In another part of the same interview, Elizabeth refers to students who are native speakers of English as "non-multilingual students." She uses this term naturally, as part of the terminology she employs when describing her students. This is important, because Elizabeth's language reverses the marginalization of multilingual students as speakers of "other" languages. It is a norm in many US schools to centralize English-speaking students. This is evident in the general assumption that students in US classrooms are proficient in English. Those who are not proficient are classified as "other."

Elizabeth chooses to resist these norms by employing the term "non-multilingual." In doing so, she centers multilingualism. This centering necessarily marginalizes English monolingualism. Not only does Elizabeth's alternative terminology refuse to perpetuate normative linguistic power structures, but she insists on a wider perspective of what could be normalized. Kaylee, like Elizabeth, narrates herself as a changemaker and a resister. She is inquisitive about her students' languages and empathetic of their experiences. See box 3.2 for Kaylee's found poem

Kaylee

I never wanted to be a teacher/Took a teaching course/Really fell in love with teaching//Degree in international relations/Went to Ecuador/Columbia, China, South Korea/Prepared me for how hard, and draining, and exhausting it is to be a minority culture/I came back to [name of state].//Marriage of my interests/in international studies/certain gift for learning language/geography/Pushed me into teaching those from other cultures.//Students from East Africa/and Northern Triangle in Central America/Drive to work specifically with these students/

"My teacher cares about me and cares about my language,/and knows that it's important"/Because of what I teach and who I teach,/I think a lot of my students.//I'm not religious,/but I would classify as a humanist./And that seems to be very much in line/with what social justice means./That is something that defines who I am/and what decision I make daily./Humanism, to me, is the belief that I can be good/It's the belief that what I do here—now—matters/that what I should do daily is do the most good for the most people/whenever I have that opportunity.

KAYLEE'S STORY

Kaylee imagines her students might see her as caring because of her engagement with their lives and languages. This representation of Kaylee also emphasizes how she justifies her pedagogical practices. She positions herself as equipped to "be good" and to do good despite whatever context or circumstances surround her. She upholds these beliefs, not because they are tenets of a religion, but because she personally constructed this objective and set of values for herself. She describes how her beliefs influence daily actions.

Kaylee self-identifies as American, middle-class, and female. At the time of the interview, Kaylee was thirty years old. She calls herself English speaking and White. To her, the most important aspects of her identity are her race, class, and gender. She notes that being middle-class and White may be barriers to connecting with her students. She observes that her students are more likely to connect with individuals who "look and sound, with similar languages, as they do."

She also identifies as a humanist atheist. She defines humanism as the belief that a person "can be good without a higher deity. It's the belief that what I do here and now matters." Kaylee sees humanism as "very much in line with what social justice means." She describes her beliefs as personal, not necessarily grounded in broader religion but instead a set of beliefs she connects to in everyday actions and decisions. Kaylee earned an undergraduate degree in international relations, with intentions of going on to law school. However, she took a break from school and traveled to Ecuador, where she took a course on teaching English as an additional language.

That started her journey teaching English in Columbia, Ecuador, China, and South Korea before returning to the midwestern United States to earn a master's degree and license for teaching ESL. She notes that the majority of the students she taught while abroad were upper-middle–class adults. In her role as a public–high-school English language development teacher in the Midwest, she teaches newcomer refugee and displaced students. She reports that many of these families arrived from East Africa and Central America. She sees teaching English to newcomers as a connection between her interests in international studies and language learning.

Kaylee explains how she has "a certain gift" for learning languages. However, Kaylee understands that her natural ability to learn language is not enough to identify as proficient in a language. She states that she has some proficiency in Spanish but resists saying she is fluent. Instead, she emphasizes the "effort to learn" the languages of her students. She believes learning languages helps her communicate and connect with her students. It also demonstrates that she understands the challenge of learning language and, importantly, that she cares about her students' home languages.

Kaylee describes social-justice teaching as "trying to create a system that is equitable specifically for those [refugee and displaced] students"; however, she is hesitant to self-identify as a social-justice–oriented educator. She is "still trying to figure out" how her work enacts what she believes socially just education to be. However, she believes that identity [socially just teacher] is not important but rather "the outcome would be more important." The way Kaylee emphasizes outcomes and actions in social-justice teaching aligns with the way she employs the values of humanism to justify decisions and behaviors in her life. Intention or belief is not enough because action and outcome are key to the way Kaylee understands ways of being.

KAYLEE AS A CHANGEMAKER

Kaylee describes a time when she crafted and utilized alternative teaching tools to better support newcomer refugee students in a language-development reading intervention course. She created a self-paced "extremely differentiated" program to support students in developing a wide variety of reading skills. Kaylee describes how she designed materials that "meets students where they are" so that each student received the interventions and supports they needed to advance their reading abilities.

Kaylee notes that this redesign of materials was "a ton of work" but also rewarding. Many of her students of refugee backgrounds have limited or interrupted formal education. This may have caused gaps in their literacy development in their home languages, which affects literacy development in the target language, English. Because each student experienced unique opportunities to develop initial literacy skills, the skills of the students in Kaylee's reading class are varied. She was able to rethink traditional understandings about "what makes a proficient reader" and how educators can contribute to student's reading development.

By innovating resources, Kaylee imagines new ways of "flexibly and creatively" (Dal et al., 2016, p. 161) meeting and advancing her students' diverse skills. This kind of changemaking enables students, who may otherwise be disadvantaged by traditional methods of teaching reading, to pinpoint areas of growth and advance areas of strength in an adaptable and responsive classroom. In this way, her pedagogical entrepreneurship fosters a "creative atmosphere" (p. 173).

Another way Kaylee recounts changemaking is when she supported refugee newcomers beyond the classroom. In addition to being a language-development instructor, Kaylee also coaches the swim team at her school. Kaylee describes how she created opportunities and worked to remove barriers so that Muslim refugee women could join the school's swim team. The girls who joined the team, according to Kaylee, were "some of the first in the state" to enjoy the new opportunity Kaylee supported.

Kaylee notes how the Muslim team members needed "alternative swimwear" in order to participate comfortably. This swimwear necessitated a waiver, because the organization that oversees the state's high-school athletics, according to Kaylee, "had originally banned the sort of swimsuits that they need to wear." Kaylee acted flexibly and creatively (Dal et al., 2016, p. 161) in order to ensure equitable opportunity for the Somali refugee swimmers. She also supported the swimmers by providing initial swimming lessons and transportation. Here she recounts the narrative:

> In previous years, we actually had some of our young Somali women on the team, and they were some of the first in the state to be on the swim team, and we had to have a lot of additional supports in place. We had to have alternative swimwear, which included a waiver, because the state had originally banned the sort of swimsuits that they needed to wear. We had to provide initial swim lessons for them, and we had to then provide transportation for those swim lessons, and actually, from that idea there was, kind of, a genesis around, well, let's go ahead and create a whole swim camp around helping students of color make sure that they know how to swim. In the United States, drowning is, I think, the third or fourth greatest cause of accidental death of children under the ages of seven or ten. So, one of my jobs, because I'm a swim coach and because I have these gifts, I think I have a real ability to change that.

In imagining new roles refugee women can occupy, Kaylee was able to remove barriers so that students had a new opportunity. This act of advocacy exemplifies a key component of what might be possible for a teacher who takes on the role of changemaker in nontraditional spaces.

Creating opportunities for a few women on a single team was not the limit of Kaylee's vision. Eventually, this changemaking evolved into creating "a whole swim camp around helping students of color make sure that they know how to swim." The area where Kaylee teaches and coaches has a number of water areas, including fast-moving rivers and deep, cold quarries. Kaylee explains how the swimming camp she imagined was designed to address the danger of drowning in the area, especially for people who did not grow up learning to proficiently navigate the water in the area. She imagined how she could creatively work around existing barriers in order to include refugee and displaced families in learning to swim.

Kaylee represents being a changemaker in the ways she aspires to create new ways schools can meet social changes. Kaylee describes a dream educational opportunity, barring the limits of time, resources, and funds. This kind of dreaming models how changemakers' creative thinking and flexible responses can address the changing needs of educators and schools that support newcomer refugees. Kaylee thinks about alternative and additional ways she can support her students and their families holistically because she is a changemaker.

Kaylee describes the value of dual-language programs that promote multilingualism for all students. The program Kaylee envisions would include parents and families of the students in order to embrace multiple languages and perspectives simultaneously. She imagines how this kind of program would emphasize the importance of home languages and home cultures. She also imagines how an encompassing program like this could provide broader access to materials like "dental care, eye care, and mental health supports for PTSD and trauma."

Despite being limited by role and resources, Kaylee still dreams. Though it was not within her power to create various programs and curricula at the time of this interview, she still thinks creatively about what could be. By continuing to envision alternative ways of operating within a school and ways the school could support refugee and displaced students and their families beyond the school, Kaylee equips herself to be a changemaker. Resources and roles may be obstacles that block the opportunity to enact Kaylee's ideas today, but, by imagining what might be, Kaylee might someday identify ways to work around existing limits or create new opportunities.

KAYLEE AS A RESISTER

Kaylee recounts how she has resisted traditional roles in athletics in order to create opportunities for diverse students. As coach of the swim team at her school, she purposefully established "definitive roles" for herself. She did this in an effort to ensure that she was working toward "recruiting swimmers and student athletes that reflect the diversity and strengths of the school." She notices that many athletics teams, including the one she leads, are not representative of the student body as a whole. She imagines changes she can lead that may create opportunities for students who are not currently engaged in sports.

She describes how she "deliberately put a Black student, a Jewish Asian student, and an LGBTQ student in charge," with the responsibility to recruit diversely for their own swim team. She noted that she wanted to ensure "those were the faces" of the team. She imagined ways to provide opportunities for diverse students to join a team, to inhabit leadership roles, and to open this opportunity beyond "just the White middle-class students who have access to everything anyway." Kaylee's narrative demonstrates resistance because she acknowledges the ways students are normally represented in athletics, particularly swimming, and actively chooses to negate these norms through constructing specific roles in leadership and recruiting representative swimmers.

Though one swim team is a limited example, it is symbolic. As the coach, Kaylee utilized agency in the domain where she had influence. Although the alternative roles Kaylee imagines for the swim team she leads may not immediately affect how other teams operate, the leadership and resistance Kaylee models may create a ripple effect. Kaylee's swim team may serve as an alternative model to the norms of student leadership and representation, which can more broadly reduce traditional limits of involvement for diverse students in other roles.

REFLECTION

Both Elizabeth and Kaylee are changemakers and resisters. Elizabeth collaborates with co-teachers to restructure assessments to resist linguistic bias. Kaylee imagines and creates a self-paced reading intervention that can better support emergent readers. However, the nuances between them are notable and worthy of examination. This is important because there is no "one" way to practice socially just pedagogy. Teachers' unique strengths and skills deserve consideration. Just as we employ an asset-based lens for students, so, too, should we employ one for teachers.

Huat and Shunmugam (2021) present another way to view teachers as changemakers. They discuss how teacher changemakers can influence students' future employability, social position, and personal status and pathways (p. 88). Through this lens, educational changemakers not only change educational systems and strategies to better suit their students but also change the students to better fit into the existing systems.

The authors consider how this perspective of educational changemakers suggests a deficit or challenge exists innately in the learners. The authors argue that Elizabeth and Kaylee do not exhibit this kind of changemaking. Instead, they both focus on ways to transform educational practice and systemic norms in order to make room for the diverse skills, assets, and ways of being they notice in their refugee and displaced learners. They work as allies, shouldering that responsibility themselves. Elizabeth collaborates with colleagues while Kaylee forges new programs, as in her leadership of the swim team. Kaylee especially dreams of new models, such as bilingual programming and new opportunities for families, as a way of changemaking.

Elizabeth and Kaylee narrate resistance uniquely, but they both practice slowing, refusing, and negating structures that disadvantage newcomer students. Elizabeth enacts resistance by both acknowledging and denying the existing limits in her role as a public-school educator. She does not accept that the quality of her students' education is limited by the resources associated with a "free education." Instead, she insists on working beyond those limits and aspires to greater outcomes.

Elizabeth also responds to and negates the effects of systemic assumptions about her identity and her role. By exploring and identifying her privilege, power, and authority, she can then denounce it and seek an alternative liminal space. Similarly, Kaylee works to recast individuals as new alternatives to archetypal roles, as in the coaching and student leadership roles she intentionally shapes.

REFERENCES

Burridge, N., & Buchanan, J. (2022). Teachers as changemakers in an age of uncertainty. In Heggart, K., Kolber, S. (Eds). *Empowering teachers and democratizing schooling*. Springer. https://doi.org/10.1007/978-981-19-4464-2_6.

Dal, M., Elo, J., Leffler, E., Svedberg, G., & Westerberg, M. (2016). Research on pedagogical entrepreneurship—a literature review based on studies from Finland, Iceland and Sweden. *Education Inquiry*, 7(2).

Huat, C. M. & Shunmugam, K. (2021). Every teacher a changemaker: Reflections on teacher agency and empowerment. *The English Teacher*, 50(2), 85–101. https://doi.org/10.52696/fwym7144.

Jacobs, G. M., Chau, M. H., & Hamzah, N. H. (2022). Students and teachers as changemakers. *REFLections*, 29(1), 112–29.

Lyotard, J. F. (1984). *The postmodern condition*. Manchester University Press.

McInerney, Shaun. (2020). What is changemaker education?: Everyone a changemaker. *Ashoka*, www.ashoka.org/en-us/story/what-changemaker-education. Accessed 17 July 2023.

McKeon, K. A., Merchant, B., Flanagan-Gonzales, C., & Sultan, S. (2022). Thin places of resistance: A caring response to refugees in rural American schools. *Educational Review*. doi:10.1080/00131911.2022.2039593.

Chapter 4

Empathy and Agency

In this chapter, the authors explore how empathy and agency are visible in the narratives of two rural, midwestern public–high-school teachers. Steven is a history teacher, and Naomi is an ESL teacher. This chapter focuses specifically on their work with students displaced from Puerto Rico to this rural midwestern community. The authors highlight the role of critical self-reflection and the importance of dismantling barriers necessary for teachers to engage in social-justice work for displaced students and families within the community. In the following sections, the authors will define empathy and agency and then discuss how they are present in Steven's and Naomi's stories.

EMPATHY

As articulated by Sonia Nieto (2006), the need for teachers to have empathy is part of the "taken-for-granted truth that relationships are at the heart of teaching" (p. 466). Empathy may be both cognitive and emotional. Emotional empathy reflects a mirroring or feeling of another's emotions, whereas cognitive empathy recognizes an understanding of how another sees the world (Howe, 2012). Importantly, the authors emphasize the importance of human emotion, such as empathy, in the education of refugee students.

Empathy can help promote a welcoming and accepting environment for refugee students and can have an influence on attitudes and outcomes. Teaching based on empathy can promote trusting teacher-student relationships within the classroom and lead to student confidence and engagement. As Strekalova and Hoot (2008) explain, although few teachers have experienced the same hardships, "with a bit of deliberate understanding [empathy] of refugee children's pasts, teachers can play a major role in helping them carve a brighter future" (p. 21).

The development of empathy, which requires skill and practice, is a core concern of teacher education. Empathy is advanced through first understanding oneself and then learning about students. It requires that teachers are willing to be vulnerable (Sealey-Ruiz, 2022) and open themselves to the experience of others. Empathetic teachers work to gain an understanding of their students' perspectives.

Some scholars have referred to the need for *radical empathy*. Radical empathy is a deliberate and mindful action that provides a feeling of direct and deep connection with students (Ratcliffe, 2012). It begins with teachers interrogating their own lives, including their understandings and biases. It then allows them to move beyond the norms and connections of their own worlds and practice understanding and compassion (Givens, 2021). The following is posited by Sellars and Imig (2021):

> As the development of radical empathy is a deliberate, conscious [deconstruction] of personal and professional cultural cues, traditions, practices, assumptions, belief systems, and values in an attempt to be open to the participation in another's experiences and realities, it requires a dedicated systematic approach of reflection and investigation of the presumptions and taken for grantedness of our own daily lives (p. 426).

Although empathy is an important first step to being an effective social-justice educator, it is not sufficient without action. Empathy should be followed by taking action to create change.

TEACHER AGENCY

Taking action, in addition to developing empathy, requires teacher agency. A basic definition of teacher agency is "active contribution to shaping [one's] work and its conditions" (Biesta, Priestley, & Robinson, 2015, p. 624). However, teacher agency is not an individual quality in teachers but, rather, is based on what they can do within certain contexts. In other words, having agency and achieving agency is an interplay of individual efforts and intentionality and contextual factors in unique situations.

Moreover, teacher agency relies on influences from the past, future, and present. Biesta et al., (2015) elaborate as follows:

> [T]he achievement of agency is always informed by the past experience, including personal and professional biographies; that it is orientated towards the future, both with regard to more short-term and more long-term perspectives; and that it is enacted in the here-and-now, where such enactment is influenced by what refer to as cultural, material, and structural resources (p. 627).

Thus, teachers come to their ideas about taking action based on what they have experienced in the past, what they hope to achieve in the future, and what is needed and allowed in the present.

However, in the current educational environment, teacher agency is often at odds with institutional structures that do not allow for individual action. Policies often focus on the actions it takes to be an effective teacher "while ignoring or subverting the cultural and structural conditions which play an important role in enabling this to happen" (Priestly et al., 2015, p. 2). Thus, within the scope of social justice and the education of minoritized students, teachers are often positioned as change agents whose duty is to question and push against systems that hinder student efficacy.

Agent power within these contexts can be generated through reflection and evaluation of contexts. This affords teachers the ability to analyze their practices toward social justice. Pantic (2105) developed a model that sees agents as embedded in their contexts, yet capable of transforming them. In this model, teacher agency includes teachers' individual and collective sense of purpose and their ability and willingness to act and reflect on those actions in the pursuit of equitable outcomes for students.

Steven and Naomi both reflect on how they show empathy with their students. In the narratives that follow, the authors explore aspirational radical empathy within Steve and Naomi's stories and ideas about agency within their specific contexts. Steven's found poem in box 4.1 begins his story of understanding himself as he works to build connections with his students.

Steven

I'm not just a guy, I'm a big White guy/A position of privilege/And that threat is ever present// My biases are fairly strong/I have to challenge those constantly.//I'm a coach/A father figure to a lot of these guys/Middle-class growing up,/Not so much now; my life has been a train wreck.//I've lacked stability/My home, my income/I've had to worry about what comes next/But it's not something that I make public knowledge.

I try to put myself in their shoes/A strong sense of empathy is what I bring/In order to teach these kids and help these kids/I'm going to have to adjust how I do things./My door's always open/I'm there and listening to them.//I'm a dad/A dog owner/A teacher/An empathetic guy who cries during sappy Hallmark movies/There are stereotypes and labels that go with these,/But it gives a rough approximation of who I am and where I'm at.//I check all the boxes/Am I privileged in this?/Yes, I am.

STEVEN'S STORY

Steven describes himself as a lower-middle–class, White male, father, teacher, and coach. He has lived and worked the entirety of his life within one hundred miles of where he was born and raised. As the son of a pastor and an elementary teacher, Steven realizes he has more "stability and opportunity" than many of his students, simply because of his "very structured and sheltered" upbringing.

When the interviews began, Steven was in his third year as a social-studies teacher and coach in a diverse, rural high school, but in his twelfth year of teaching overall. In his career, Steven had taught in a number of schools ranging from a charter school for students in recovery to a suburban school outside a large metropolitan area. Each of these jobs was for a short stint, because either the school closed or his "life choices" forced a change. At the conclusion of the interviews, Steven had completed his fifth year in the school, and he found that that afforded him more voice and agency in the system.

Steven earned a bachelor's degree in social-studies education from a midwestern state college, although he began his postsecondary education at a small, private, religiously affiliated college. There, he felt like he stood out as being lower economically than others, which helped him understand how it is not to fit in based on factors beyond his control. Currently holding a steady job as a teacher and providing for his family, he notes that his life has been a "train wreck" due to personal and professional instability and transience. Yet, he still identifies as privileged as he knows that privilege is not just economic.

He recognizes that his life experiences have contributed to his perceptions about social justice. Steven's reflections about his identities enable us to see how he believes others perceive him. While imposing in stature, he is a self-proclaimed "big, White guy," who "cries during sappy Hallmark movies." Steven goes beyond recognizing how his various identities exist as stereotypes; he unpacks how these identities develop, admitting that being who he is brings a position of privilege. The elements in his history shape how he engages with his students, and he balances that with intentionality in his pedagogical choices and a strong sense of empathy.

EMPATHY IN STEVEN'S NARRATIVES

In his narratives, Steven reveals how empathy is a part of his ideals related to social-justice education. Reflecting on his work with refugee and displaced students, as well as his work with other marginalized students, Steven explains how his own background and experience open him to connect with and better understand his responsibilities to their education and care. Steven shows emotional empathy when he tells about a time that he cried for "kids in timeout when [he worked] in daycare." He also shows cognitive empathy when he talks about his need to to understand how others see the world.

First, Steven reflects on his own background and how he interrogates his understandings and biases in order to open himself up to the experience of others. He discusses his awareness that who he is brings him a certain privilege in society. His identity as a White, middle-class man of large stature brings him a position of power in many contexts, including school:

> So, I think it also is how I see myself. I mean, when I think of who I am, number one, is a teacher, but being a man is going to have certain things come with it that would be different if I was a woman. Being White is very different. It's that position of privilege, and it's going to be very different than if it would be if I were a person of color. Middle class is very different than if I was rich or poor. It's just going to give a different world view . . . Again, they could be stereotypes and labels, but I think they can give someone a rough approximation of who I am and where I'm at, and we get to know each other from there.

Steven then compares his life experiences with those of his students, beginning with his early teaching in schools with students experiencing poverty and other life challenges. He draws on his own background with transience and financial insecurity to connect with and understand his students' basic needs. "My life hasn't been super successful in terms of finances, which helps in this case; I can put myself in their shoes a little bit," Steven admits. He also moved around often in his childhood, which helps him to understand those stresses. In his personal and professional life, Steven has felt unsettled and disconnected himself at times.

However, Steven's deliberate and sometimes uncomfortable work to build understanding and see the world as his students do requires that he be vulnerable about his own identity and experiences. He critically reflects on how he sees himself and how that vision changes based on his experiences with his students and their lives. For instance, Steven discusses his realization that "the talk" his father had with him was not the same talk that young men of color receive about interactions with police and "that shook [him]." Steven narrates how, although he has had some similar experiences, he knows that those of his students have been traumatic in ways he may never fully understand:

> And so just understanding and challenging this idea that my perception of reality is what everybody else's is and understanding that it's not. And even though I might have some hardships from time to time, not that those are any more or less valid than others, but it's not the same. Everyone's coming at it from a different point of view, and it's something I try to teach in history anyway. It's just

as good to have it reinforced and to keep challenging myself and making sure that I remember that.

Steven's empathetic nature is demonstrated in his humility and compassion. He discloses his concern and fear for what his students may have been experiencing in the greater community.

It was through his early work that Steven began his journey towards social-justice teaching. He narrates that he was "thrown into the fire right away, working with a lot of students who were [experiencing poverty]." He adds, "[I] didn't understand what poor meant" until then. He tried to make adjustments to his practice based on his growing awareness, admitting that he "was not overly successful [his] first couple of years." He claims, "But I kept working."

During those years, followed by his current experience working in a school with many displaced students, Steven has tried to build trust with his students as he finds that relationships are "the key to unlocking that desire to learn," which in turn promotes a safe, welcoming environment. He makes a point to get to know his students and reach out to engage them in and outside the classroom, finding out what they enjoy and about their interests. If students know that he is interested in understanding their experiences, it might create buy-in for his subject matter, but, importantly, students know that his class is a "safe space for them."

Steven also comments that the pedagogical choices he makes build confidence for students. For instance, he individually guides student learning through presentations and oral reports in the target language (English). He states that this strategy "helps them build confidence in the language without a large audience." He has also built up classroom materials in English and Spanish (e.g., schedules, signs, etc.). He makes sure to celebrate success, no matter how small the accomplishment.

While these intentions may not be unique to Steven, they are emblematic of someone who knows the importance of feeling a sense of belonging in order to invest academically and emotionally. In addition, Steven shares how his curriculum and pedagogies changed with the additional disconnection between the displaced students and his curriculum. As a social-studies teacher, Steven comments, there are plenty of opportunities to bring in student background and voice; the challenge for him exists in being responsive and not triggering something in the students' past. Steven prides himself in highlighting the experiences and history reflected in the demographics of his class.

For instance, when teaching about the New Deal, Steven remembers how he encouraged students to look at projects that addressed needs within the students' own backgrounds. For the displaced students from Puerto Rico, this included the Puerto Rican Reconstruction Administration:

We try to find ways to incorporate what we're talking about so it's not just great White men history . . . I do a New Deal project every year, and they have to choose . . . One of them that I found is a minor thing in most textbooks [Puerto Rican Reconstruction Administration], if it's there at all, but a lot of stuff happens. And so I always put that as one of the options and inevitably, oh, we're doing that one. It's like, "Oh, it's my home. I can talk about it." And then they can see that sense of pride that, "Well, this is where I'm from." And they can add that and they can talk about, "I've been here." And there's something to that where, just as a history teacher, it's like, "Oh, if I've been there, it helps. I can give that little extra." And they can do that. And then that really lifts up everybody else.

According to Steven, students enjoy connecting their homes to the curriculum. He believes that it "validates who they are and where they were from." He adds how important it is for all students to see their peers' histories as interesting and valuable.

Curricular choices such as those offered by Steven help to dismantle stereotyping. He recalls how he helped build empathy among all the students in the class. One of his Dominican students told the class about his family's long road to get US citizenship, which helped other students understand the experience:

And just to see the wide eyes of all the people who had no idea and to see that click like, "Oh, this is real, he's had to go through a lot to get here. What does that actually mean? Whereas I get to take this for granted." And I think that was meaningful just because you get to see one, he got to tell a story, which was neat. [Student's name] is just a great kid anyway, but you got to tell the story and then to see everybody else understand that and learn from it.

This empathy extends to outside the classroom, where Steven recalls some of his players standing up for their Puerto Rican teammates against racism in the community.

Finally, COVID-19 pandemic protocols brought about a significant change in Steven's perceptions of teaching and care. As students were at home, learning remotely, Steven was also at home teaching remotely. He found himself struggling to keep his "privilege hidden" and accepting that "his students didn't often show up for synchronous classes or show themselves on screen due to their circumstances." He shares how he has been "challenging this idea that [his] perception of reality is what everybody else's is and understanding that it is not." Steven insists that his commitment to diversity and his practice of empathy has to begin with constantly "challenging [him]self."

Throughout Steven's narratives, we see examples of his empathy and his growth towards radical empathy. By first understanding and examining his own experiences through self-reflection and then using those understandings to critically position the lives of his students, Steven has worked to act on ways to improve his own teaching practice. He explains, "A strong sense of empathy is what I bring. That only goes so far, but it then leads to a desire to make sure the kids have what they need."

According to Steven, however, "[T]he opposite of empathy is apathy, and it's very easy to become apathetic." In the next section, we can see examples of Steven's desire to help students get what they need in the context of societal and institutional structures that may help or hinder the realization of his actions. His desire to act is seen within the construct of teacher agency.

AGENCY IN STEVEN'S NARRATIVES

In the first interview, Steven reflects on how he sees himself as a social-justice educator, distinguishing equity as "giving students what they need to succeed." He discusses how the current system is "not necessarily acknowledging the demographic realities coming in the near future" and, to some extent, already present in his school. The diversification of the PK–12 student body will require changes in educator perspectives, and, while he realizes "it's easier just to get by [with the status quo]," he also acknowledges that "I feel like this could be a chance to do something bold."

Steven's response is foundational to the ideas of what make systems effective in working with students who enter educational systems as displaced or refugee students. It begins with teachers, like Steven, who demonstrate purpose, willingness, and competence. Steven's broad experience in his teaching career has allowed him to see his role in the greater systems more clearly. Steven's "willingness to experiment with new methods to better meet the needs of [his] students" and deep commitment to a positive school atmosphere (Pantic, 2015, p. 768) is a hallmark of his daily practice. He is willing to do what is needed for students to be successful.

While he envisions himself as knowledgeable and aware of the societal forces that impact the refugee and displaced students in his classroom, he hedges on his ability to push against systemic issues. He wonders, "How do we challenge the systemic structures that limit what we do?" He mentions certain societal and institutional factors that may slow or prevent change.

> What do we do there? I think that while I and other teachers have a desire to change things, systemically it becomes problematic in how we do things and running into those roadblocks. I think they could be overcome, and we continue to work on that, but it also makes things go very slowly.

Steven specifically points to "people in small towns . . . school boards demanding their teachers not teach critical race theory when no teacher there teaches critical race theory and never has. But they're calling for people's heads." So he admits to not bringing up some issues as much as he could since he fears his beliefs and action might cost him his job: "We were told by the superintendent down there, no controversial issues. We don't teach controversy. You just teach the facts. And if the facts are controversial, you don't teach those either is what it boiled down to."

Thus, while Steven is able to demonstrate individual agency within the contexts of his classroom and coaching, on school, district, and community levels, he feels his agency is limited. He, however, thinks about possibilities and his vision if he were given greater voice within the system.

> I'd like to say I would fight tooth and nail, and I'd like to say that, and I hope I would, but I think, it's one of those things that until you're put in that spot, until you see the building burning, you don't know if you're going to run in. And I'd like to think I would. I hope I'm that person. And I try to be. I practice at it but.

Steven speaks to his willingness and sense of purpose to act, looking toward the possibility of future results, but wonders what he can do in the here and now:

> And I think, pushing back against, I'm sure you've run into it, I know you've run into it, just the system. I think about those old, "Why don't you ask the man?" But, it really is hard to push against . . . But it's just trying to push against that. It's difficult. Saying, "Okay, well what's the right thing to do? How can we do it?" It keeps chipping away . . . if you don't have radicals, nothing changes . . . I'm more of a consensus bringer . . . but I played the role of radical too, and it bit me when I was first teaching, so that was tough.

Change isn't just about ability and willingness but also about what can be done in the current context. He is conflicted. He asks, "Do you lead a revolution or just try to get kids to pass?" Steven considers his position on the school's leadership team and the complexity of systems change. He notes that they will always be "running into roadblocks," but the key is to "either find workarounds or challenge [the roadblocks] directly."

Steven notes that it's just trying to "push against that it's difficult." He adds, "Okay, well what's the right thing to do? How can we do it? [I] keep chipping away." Steven mentions that he feels there are veteran teachers whose voices are heard over those of others, but he has learned that, when he wants to make a change, he finds the workarounds when necessary. When that doesn't work, he leans into the experience, advice, and partnership of veteran teachers to have his ideas move forward.

Like Steven, Naomi is a teacher with years of experiences in diverse classrooms that shape her perspectives on teaching. See box 4.2 for Naomi's found poem. Through her own words, Naomi builds empathy and agency. Her narrative is different from Steven's, but she still works to better support refugee and displaced students. She uses her sense of social justice to shape her classroom environment.

Naomi

I'm from a small town and a century family farm/Family identity is pretty strong/Everyone is close/We all moved away, and we all came back/Pretty specific gender roles/They don't value my opinion, but they value me/The injustice of it has made me more aware.//I'm an ESL teacher/Started in California, five years/I knew nobody/Then came back home/To teach in an elementary school/Took a year off to learn more Spanish/To be more equipped to communicate better with parents/Moved to Guatemala not knowing a soul/Then to Mexico without connections

I believe in having more empathy/When things seem strange/When things get hard/And feel weird/Because being in a place that is not your home is difficult enough./We take so many things for granted//I'm meant to help people/This is where God wants me to be/To keep going even when it's difficult/I can't fix everything, but I can make some things better/This is where I'm supposed to be

NAOMI'S STORY

Naomi describes herself as a White, Christian woman, a veteran ESL teacher, and a small-town community member. She highlights her strong connection to home and family. She grew up on a "farm that has been in her family for over one hundred years" and is a "daughter and sister bonded by geography and values." Naomi's deep connections and feelings about home and family influence her perceptions of her students and their experiences..

Naomi worked as an elementary teacher for five years before becoming an ESL teacher. She has been in her current position for almost two decades. Despite living the majority of her life in two rural, largely homogeneous midwestern counties, she moved to California in order to find a teaching job following her teacher preparation. When she decided to return home, an ESL teaching position in this rural midwestern setting opened and she accepted it.

She then earned her teaching license in TESL. According to Naomi, it was an opportunity to pursue a "greater design for her life."

Naomi narrates that her experiences have broadened her cultural understandings. She pushes herself into "the unfamiliar" in order to learn and grow personally and professionally. In her position, she is responsible for building her students' language skills, and she finds that she is also a significant resource for parents and families. Because she felt a strong ethical obligation to do a better job of the latter, Naomi took a sabbatical from teaching to develop her Spanish speaking skills. After spending a year in Guatemala and Mexico, Naomi returned more aware of her agency as a Spanish speaker at her school.

Naomi's dedication to family and language acquisition is evident in her work and reflections. She recognizes how important feelings of safety and belonging are for both students and parents. She values her ability to be a bridge to safety, belonging, and community for her students and their families. Naomi admits that the language barrier refugees and displaced students and families face limits accessibility and agency; however, she firmly believes that she is positioned and able to be a catalyst for change and opportunity.

EMPATHY IN NAOMI'S NARRATIVES

In her narratives, Naomi takes a personal and professional journey to understand how her own beliefs, biases, experiences, and practices have shifted over time. Naomi's perceptions are deeply embedded in her understandings of home, language, and community. The biases she holds and sees in others are framed by traditional midwestern conservative ethics; however, she vulnerably divulges small, meaningful actions demonstrating empathy and creating change. She knows she is in a unique position to see what others cannot and affect change in ways that others cannot access.

Naomi's strong sense of belonging to a place—where she grew up and later returned—has helped her to try to interpret belonging for her students. She strives to understand how they see the world at the same time that she appreciates that place may not mean the same things to them as it does to her:

> Maybe [they don't] have that sense of belonging to [this] place. Maybe they have it, it's just not where they belong. That's who you are. I guess in that sense, I can say, "Oh yeah, I get that. Also, despite the very cold weather this week, I'm here by choice. This is a good place to be. This can be a good place for you. I don't know how that all works out for them."

She continues by discussing that belonging is an elusive idea, defined by people in different ways.

Naomi's desire to understand her students better by opening up to the experiences of others motivated her to travel to Guatemala and Mexico to learn Spanish. She wanted to "feel better equipped to communicate with parents." This experience not only gave her some language skills but also enabled her to experience learning a language and encountering unfamiliar places and things. She proposes that having such experiences is not equivalent to being a displaced person but that having these "experiences [gave] me more empathy than had I not lived or been to different places." Her steps, in her view, are deliberate steps to possibly see how others encounter the world.

Naomi admits that in the several years preceding the arrival of the displaced students and their families, she had not had to think much about transitioning from one culture to another. Her students at the time were largely children from Mexican-immigrant families who were already members, at least to some extent, of the community. In supporting her new students from Puerto Rico and the Dominican Republic, Naomi drew on her experiences in California, Guatemala, and Mexico where she felt "things are going to seem strange" and where she "didn't know anything about where [she] was." With this reminder, she recalls a shift in how she addressed the safety, security, and language needs of her displaced students and their families.

Naomi consistently frames the ways she serves students in terms of their sense of safety and security, connecting their sense of place and school as an extension of home. Naomi describes the challenges she experiences in helping her students and their parents adjust to environmental and situational differences. Not only is the climate significantly different, but also the ways families engage with schools are different. She is adamant, however, that engagement with families is key to students' success. Naomi's emphasis on family may, in fact, come from her own close ties to her family:

> I guess I'm interested in supporting students and their families because I think that families influence children the most. If we don't support families, we're not supporting the whole student, because there's so much beyond. They're only with us a little time. Some of my students I see for thirty minutes a day . . . so, if there are ways to support the parents and the families, I'm a very strong advocate for that.

Naomi believes she was intitally unprepared for the barrage of calls and visits from parents about winter clothing, bringing leftovers to school for lunch, and expressing concern about how the children were treated in school. Reflecting on this, Naomi resolved that there were missteps she and the administration made to ensure a clearly articulated and comfortable transition for the displaced children and their families to the school and community. Naomi articulates that the parents wanted assurance that their children were safe and cared for. They "needed to see we had a plan," she adds. "They needed to see that their children would be valued and cared for."

Naomi's beliefs about feeling valued in a space go back to her childhood. The stinging reminder of feeling unheard shifted her attitudes and actions. She remembers that, as a girl in a conservative family, she also felt unheard. She reflects that "maybe the injustice of it has made me more aware." However, Naomi also acknowledges that the injustices faced by marginalized students are rooted in deeper, societal-level constructs:

> Because of my job, a lot of it has to do with helping them learn English skills so they can stand up for themselves or make sure the people aren't taking advantage of them. Our curriculum continues to point out the inequalities that [are] in our country.

As a teacher of ESL, Naomi's perspective about language acquisition changed through the course of her career. She shares that she initially believed "language is a means to an end." She has more recently reconsidered how much language is tied to identity. She reinforces how language, family, and identity are intertwined. In "our" community, "English is the language of power." She qualifies her statement with the idea that "a personal power comes from where you come from." For her displaced students, Naomi has learned that it is not only family and language but also their experience that is powerful.

AGENCY IN NAOMI'S NARRATIVES

As an advocate for language learners and their families, Naomi demonstrates what agency looks like in her school. Driven by a purpose that extends beyond herself, she engages in practices that develop student agency and reflect the broader contexts students come from. Naomi encourages possibility and challenges limitations and complacency, ultimately having an impact on the practices and structures that hinder and support the refugee and displaced students and families in her school and community. Throughout the interviews, Naomi articulates a change in her capacity as a practitioner of social justice.

Naomi situates herself in the position of being a helper to others in her school, whether that be for students, parents, or peers. She frequently references her intentions to be an assistant, guide, or catalyst for others to become self-sufficient, find their strengths, or reach their potential. Naomi does not shy from this responsibility as it is one that has come from her own background and experience. She knows what it feels like to need help and not be able to access it, and she is thankful for the times she received help without asking. Naomi believes that the empathy she expresses manifests in a deep desire to help others.

As someone with longevity in the school system and within the community of English language learners, Naomi realizes she has become a resource for refugee and displaced families. Naomi explains how the Spanish language connection enabled her to develop trusting relationships with displaced families, coworkers, and neighbors from Mexico more quickly. She recalls how she has become "approachable by transference." When adults who had been her students can share that she has expertise that can be passed on to newcomers, she is a safe, comfortable resource. People "trust me because of my longevity," she states.

That familiarity has provided opportunities for Naomi to see the broader forces at play for displaced students. She finds herself dismantling her own biases and beliefs. Challenging her own assumptions and personal history, Naomi works to advocate against racism and discrimination. She checks her own biases, asking "Is this right? Am I thinking about this fairly?" She also challenges others to do the same.

Naomi is conscious of how her students may be perceived in this small community. While she sees the deep need for students to maintain their home language, others in the school and community do not. She comments, "We just want them to feel safe and have the environment where they feel like they can learn."

Moving others to change their beliefs about multilingual learners is sometimes a struggle for Naomi. She is adamant:

> They [students] need people to value them as a person and as a person with a lot of potential. Sometimes people are like, "Well, they don't know anything." But they know all kinds of stuff. They know so much, it's just that they don't know English! They need people to value the things that they have to start with. They're not just an empty body waiting to learn English so they can show their abilities.

Thus, essential to her efforts in changing minds about language learning is challenging deficit mindsets. She asserts that she is working hard to help her peers see the resilience, hope, and strength the students and their families bring to the school and community.

Naomi's agency developed throughout her teaching, but nothing pushed her forward in this respect more than the COVID-19 pandemic. Naomi recalls how she found herself challenging other teachers' pedagogical choices during periods of remote learning as a means to advocate for students' success.

When students were receiving undifferentiated assignments, Naomi pushed back against her peers, who replied, "You're creating more work for us!" That didn't stop her from continuing to advocate:

> So I think sometimes, if they're a language learner, it's like, [other teachers think] "Oh, they'll [ESL teachers will] take care of it, and I don't need to change." So that's maybe the challenge for me, that I see for students because if everyone's not working toward helping the student, we're not doing as much as we could.

Teaching during the pandemic opened Naomi's eyes to different ways she could change systems to support her students. She collaborated with administration members to provide language learners one-to-one conversational English lessons with educational assistants virtually and daily. Now, after the pandemic, Naomi continues to look for opportunities to provide more practice for students. She adds, "It's about thinking creatively and outside of ourselves for what is best for our students' growth."

Empowering her students through English-language learning and lessons in self-advocacy, Naomi hopes students will "be able to grow up and have a job and be a successful part of the community." She celebrates the gifts, talents, and experiences students bring to the classroom so they see how valued they are. Ultimately, Naomi hopes her students will use those talents and skills to help others as she has done for them.

REFLECTION

Steven and Naomi share stories and experiences that demonstrate their development of empathy and agency as teachers. These episodic narratives provide insights into their shifting understandings of their own identities, pedagogies, and practices. Both engage in an excavation of their identities, backgrounds, experiences, and biases as related to their work with refugee and displaced students. Both Steven and Naomi reveal experiences in their personal and professional pasts that filtered differently and emerge with new understandings that they applied to future experiences.

Steven's reflection heightened his empathy and classroom practices. Naomi's uncovered biases and hastened development of her professional agency. Both possess a greater awareness of how their choices impact others. Not unlike those in the greater context of this study, the vulnerable and sometimes uncomfortable reflection encouraged a better and more critical understanding of the experiences of the displaced and refugee students (McAllister & Irvine, 2002).

Critical reflection that enables movement toward educational transformation is embedded in the frameworks of *radical empathy* (Givens, 2021) and the *archeology of self* (Price-Dennis & Sealey-Ruiz, 2021). In both structures, participants engage in a "steady and deep excavation" (Price-Dennis & Sealey-Ruiz, 2021, p. 26) of their own identities, histories, experiences, biases, ideas, and practices. Furthermore, the reflective process is about norms and how we educate ourselves about who we are and our own histories. In doing so, we can turn a corner to "practice understanding and compassion for the experiences of [others]" (Givens, 2021, p. 31). According to Gorski and Dalton (2020), "critical reflection can strengthen educators' agency as advocates of justice-oriented change" (p. 359).

Through Steven's narratives, the authors share examples of empathy and growth towards radical empathy. By first understanding and examining his own experiences through self-reflection, and then using those understandings to critically position the lives of his students, Steven improves his teaching practice. He explains, "A strong sense of empathy is what I bring. That only goes so far, but it then leads to a desire to make sure the kids have what they need."

Naomi, similarly, understands and empathizes with students and their families. Deciding to leave the comfort and familiarity of her home to immerse herself in Spanish-speaking communities, Naomi ventured to gather the skills and confidence she needed. Naomi recognizes the challenges her students face. To a certain extent, she is experientially able to validate the "strange" and "hard" her students are now experiencing. Ultimately, Naomi sees her investment in her students as a moral imperative.

Throughout the interviews, it became clear that Steven and Naomi examine their agency, both individually and within the system. They aspire towards radical empathy. Each of these teachers demonstrates compassion, kindness, and generosity toward the displaced students who enter their classrooms. Although they have very different journeys, they self-reflect upon their own backgrounds and intentions and articulate how they see themselves as change agents and social-justice practitioners. These are important facets of engaging in agency (Priestly et al., 2015).

Finally, both Steven and Naomi express a strong desire to change systems to better serve their students. Naomi shares ideas to improve her own classroom and interactions with students and families, while Steven focuses more on larger systems and his own experience in it. Naomi's reflective process helps her agency bloom as she gains confidence in pushing her peers to reconsider how they are serving multilingual learners. Likewise, Steven actively models empathy for his students even as he expresses how little agency he feels within the larger system.

REFERENCES

Biesta, G., Priestley, M., & Robinson, S. (2015). The role of beliefs in teacher agency. *Teachers and Teaching, 21*(6), 624–40.

Givens, T. E. (2021). *Radical empathy: Finding a path to bridging racial divides.* Bristol University Press.

Howe, D. (2012). *Empathy: What it is and why it matters.* Bloomsbury Publishing.

McAllister, G., & Irvine, J. J. (2002). The role of empathy in teaching culturally diverse students: A qualitative study of teachers' beliefs. *Journal of Teacher Education, 53*(5), 433–43. https://doi.org/10.1177/002248702237397.

Nieto, S. (2006). Solidarity, courage and heart: What teacher educators can learn from a new generation of teachers. *Intercultural Education, 17*(5), 457–73.

Pantic, N. (2015). A model for the study of teacher agency for social justice. *Teachers and Teaching, 21*(6), 759–78.

Priestley, M., Biesta, G. J. J., & Robinson, S. (2015). Teacher agency: What is it and why does it matter? In R. Kneyber & J. Evers (Eds.), *Flip the system: Changing education from the bottom up.* Routledge.

Sealey-Ruiz, Y. (2022). An archaeology of self for our times. *English Journal, 111*(5), 21–26.

Sellars, M. & Imig, S. (2021). School leadership, reflective practice, and education for students with refugee backgrounds: A pathway to radical empathy. *Intercultural Education, 32*(4), 417–29. doi: 10.1080/14675986.2021.1889988.

Strekalova, E., & Hoot, J. L. (2008). What is special about special needs of refugee children?: Guidelines for teachers. *Multicultural Education, 16*(1), 21–24.

Chapter 5

Vulnerability and Overcoming Challenges

In this chapter, the authors explore vulnerability and the ways in which two urban, northeastern public-school teachers, Emily and Nicole, narrate overcoming challenges in their roles as teachers of English learners who come from refugee and displaced backgrounds. The authors argue that it is, indeed, these teachers' vulnerability that fosters their abilities to creatively overcome a myriad of challenges, especially during the COVID-19 pandemic.

VULNERABILITY

It is important to begin with the idea that vulnerability is a strength rather than a liability or a weakness. It is an asset inherent in the teaching and learning process and the development of socially just and equity-focused pedagogies. The authors agree with scholars who write that teachers must "experience the joys and delights as well as the discomforts and tensions of vulnerability and uncertainty" (Dale & Frye, 2009, p. 124) as part of consciousness-raising.

While the authors acknowledge the importance of recognizing, honoring, and more explicitly rewarding teacher expertise and knowledge, we also caution against the idea that completion of teacher education requirements or a number of years in the field signifies a teacher's expertise or mastery in his or her field in all areas. Learning to teach is a lifelong process, especially within rapidly shifting global contexts.

To be vulnerable is to "share, co-learn, and admit you don't know" (Brantmeier, 2013, p. 3). Teachers like Emily and Nicole have an openness to being wrong. In their practices, vulnerability includes a willingness to be in and navigate situations in which they are the unknowing and uncomfortable person. Vulnerability allows educators to realize and accept the truth about themselves. It is necessary for organizational health, cooperation, and long-lasting, outstanding life endeavors. It fosters a sense of community and promotes a work environment optimized for productivity and teamwork (Gibson & Manuel, 2003).

OVERCOMING CHALLENGES

In the face of the many challenges that teachers of refugee and displaced students confront on a daily basis in US schools, Emily and Nicole display Beghetto's (2021) "creative confidence" and "creative risk-taking." They take "creative actions" to reap the benefits of "creative outcomes" (pp. 3–4) within their school communities. These challenges were further compounded by the COVID-19 pandemic during the time of the research interviews. Although educational crises are challenging and anxiety-inducing, they can also spur innovative thinking and creative solutions at and beyond the individual level (Cohen and Cromwell, 2020). At such pivotal moments, new ways of thought, action, and leadership are needed.

It is safe to say that the COVID-19 pandemic harmed school communities across the globe and caused teachers to feel unprepared and lonely. In Emily and Nicole's contexts, refugee and displaced families struggled with language barriers, access to technology, heightened fear of the unknown, and economic needs. It is well known that the pandemic heightened concerns about the effects of socioeconomic status on increasing educational disparities during the pandemic.

However, it is also safe to say that the pandemic catalyzed positive change, allowing teachers to collaborate and help one another, students to gain access to technology, and teachers to learn about and use as many tools as possible to make things work for their students. For example, significant constraints on mobility outside the house heightened the need for other methods of communication, such as video conferencing (Watson, Lupton, & Michael, 2021). Such technologies have since burgeoned and enabled a new and emerging educational landscape.

Education technology companies generously provided access to resources that allowed teachers to learn and implement new tools and pedagogies. This generosity allowed teachers to supplement instruction, facilitate long-distance teaching, and provide multiple platforms for communication and collaboration among teachers and students. This was a reassuring, unifying experience during challenging times.

In the rest of this chapter, the authors will discuss how Emily and Nicole accepted their vulnerability and practiced from a place of self-awareness, humility, agency, innovative spirit, and determination to creatively overcome challenges. The next section will discuss Emily's narratives through this framework. See box 5.1 for a portrait of Emily in her own words—a found poem constructed by the authors from the interview transcripts.

> Emily
> A White, upper-middle-class woman. I got the luck of the draw!/Only my ninth year in the game, and I'm 43 . . . /A super-zealous Roman Catholic convert./My husband is a Mexican immigrant. I love to go to Mexico./[But] I don't speak Spanish. I don't have the confidence [there]./It terrifies me. I cling to him./It furthers my appreciation for immigrants and refugees./My biggest thing[s] . . . /My Empathy . . . / Curiosity . . . /Flexibility/A genuine respect and appreciation for what they bring.//
> ESL sounds fascinating . . . Sign me up!/Then that is my vocation . . . that I have to do. Everyone assumes they're fine . . . /I really want to do right by these kids but I'm afraid I really don't know what I'm doing/Concerned with the growth of self . . . /Get their names recognized . . . /The most beautiful memories . . . /"I wish I could try Thanksgiving."/ "This is what heaven is like!"

EMILY'S STORY

In her own words, Emily is a White, middle-class, middle-aged (forty-three), English-speaking woman who had been teaching for nine years at the time of the interview. Emily earned her undergraduate degree with a double major in theater and communications. She then went on to earn a master of arts in teaching secondary English.

Realizing her privilege, Emily believes that the opportunities she has been afforded in life require her to use her position to "get someone else to a better spot." If she does not use her education and position, then "they're wasted tools." She is a Roman Catholic who believes that "God put her where she is to help others." However, Emily's respect for her students' identities is paramount to her. This is especially true of her Muslim and Hindu students, whose right to religious freedom is "incredibly important" to her.

She teaches at an urban, northeastern public elementary school where, according to her, most members of the ESL population are refugee students. These populations shift continuously as resettlement patterns change. In addition, she has taught middle-school English and in a gifted-and-talented program. These experiences motivated her to seek her ESL licensure through a state-run online program. Although she has taught at highly resourced schools, she moved quickly to the schools with students with higher needs, saying about the previous school, "[I]t just wasn't my population. They were wonderful kids, I loved them, they weren't mine."

Emily's strengths include "empathy, curiosity about other cultures, and flexibility." Emily strives to create a welcoming community in her classroom by connecting with parents, inviting families, and sharing food around holidays like Thanksgiving. Attempting to build connections with her students, she draws on her own experiences of traveling to Mexico. Due to language barriers, Emily is "terrified" of not being able to communicate and recognizes the extent to which she must "cling to others" to survive.

This experience helps her appreciate not only the struggles her students from refugee backgrounds face but also what they bring with them to the classroom; she has developed a "genuine respect and appreciation for what [immigrants] bring" and for their "incredible tenacity and strength beyond normal courage and sacrifices." She felt their pain and shared her vulnerability in developing her ability to fully support them.

VULNERABILITY IN EMILY'S NARRATIVES

Emily describes herself as feeling like "a letdown" and that she was "flying blind" when starting her role as an elementary ESL teacher. In her interview, she reports that her cohort was the last group of teachers for whom the state did not require ESL field experiences prior to receiving the license. She recognizes this as a vulnerability. She says, "I think it is a much better program now. Now the state requires that [they] have actual classroom time and things like that. That was not required when I got it." She rationalizes her choice to pursue the license and admits she felt like "a letdown for [the kids] for the first year":

> I got a job out of it, and I love where I am, but I feel like I don't have the elementary skills. I'm trying to learn them on the fly. As a middle-school English teacher, I never had to teach somebody how to read. And while I have this great curriculum that I'm using and everything, I don't have a lot of those skills. So I've been learning them with my kids. I feel like this is the first year where I'm like, "I get it now. Okay, I'm ahead of the kids." I feel like I was a letdown for them for the first year.

Although she has started to feel "more like a teacher," where she finally feels like she's "kind of hitting [her] stride" and she's more able to anticipate her students' needs, Emily acknowledges that there's still "a huge learning curve." She says, "At this point, mostly I still feel like a student." This shows her vulnerability in realizing and accepting the truth about her abilities and her lack of knowledge at any given time, while also acknowledging that learning to teach is a lifelong process and that she has to continuously work to overcome these deficits.

This example points to the joys and delights along with the discomforts and tensions of vulnerability—admitting what she doesn't know and being willing to co-learn to achieve her goals. Emily presents her position of privilege as also being an element in vulnerability since it positions her as an unknowing party—one who perhaps can never really know what it is like to be in their situation. She narrates,

> But then I think the biggest limitation we all have is it's impossible for those of us who have always lived in this country and this circumstance to ever truly understand where they are coming from. And so I am often hesitant to approach because I don't want to come off as being "White savior-y" or I don't want to come off as being over like, "Oh I know so much let me help you." I worry so much about that but sometimes I feel like I don't engage my families enough because I'm worried about going to the other extreme, if that makes sense. I know that sounds crazy. And so I'm often, this year I've made a much bigger effort to reach out more. And I'm really pleasantly surprised at the reaction that I'm getting.

Emily acknowledges that there are new things to learn as the years change and refugees from different countries arrive in her district. She narrates that "every year I find out more of what I don't know." Although she tries to be involved with local community and religious organizations to learn about her students, Emily concedes that "when you work with another culture, it's like you're wearing glasses that try to match their lens, but you can never actually see it through their eyes. You can only see it through your own interpretation and your own lenses."

Again, we see Emily's vulnerability in her acceptance of what she can't know, her concessions about her own privilege, and her finding that it is reasonable that she may have to learn more to best support her students and their families. As she says, "[T]here's so many times, again, like good intentions where I'm like, 'Oh, we need to do this for them.' And then it's like, 'Oh, that's not what they wanted at all.'"

Without this acceptance and vulnerability, Emily may make poor choices as a teacher who does not take into account the needs and viewpoints of her students. In fact, her vulnerability and discomfort spurred her into making some notable actions to improve her practice and the practice of others. She discusses how she "broke down" worrying about not supporting her students well but took action to remedy that situation:

I don't know, I feel like people like [Name] are great at going to [the state capitol] and doing these—my opinion isn't worth very much, like I don't have much to stand on, but what I can do is advocate for my kids within my school and I can advocate for my teachers to try to do the right thing and provide them with the skills that they need because most of them want to do right by the ESL kids but are afraid they're doing it wrong or don't know how to do it or think they don't know how to do it but really they have the skills. So that's where my activism comes in I think. So I called [Name] and just basically broke down on the phone and was like, "I don't know what I'm doing. How do I not screw these children up?" And she and I and a few people from [different organizations in the city] and just different people put together the Professional Learning Community for ESL teachers and I was part of the inaugural class for that because I wanted to learn. And so that was kind of how I started learning more about the craft.

OVERCOMING CHALLENGES IN EMILY'S NARRATIVES

Emily discusses overcoming many challenges, from the beginning of her career working with students from refugee backgrounds and through the pandemic. For instance, since feeling like she was "flying blind" during her first years as an ESL teacher, she has overcome those challenges to some extent and has grown to anticipate students' needs and now realizes that schools have several limitations in understanding the background of ESL students.

In some cases, Emily has had to take risks and come up with creative actions to ensure positive outcomes for her students, which demonstrates a growing confidence in her ability to be an effective teacher and advocate for her students. She has criticized standards, assessments, and test-driven curricula, which may ignore the richness of students' lives. She has also taken it upon herself to act against popular opinion to protect her students and families.

For instance, she has defended her students' right to their identities, calling out other teachers who do not bother to learn students' names: "I fight with one teacher who feels that, when the names are too hard, she just gives them nicknames, like she'll call Azra, 'Jenny,' and she's like, 'it's a funny joke we have.' I'm like, 'It's not a funny joke; it's bullshit and you are completely stripping them of their identity and that is not fair.'"

In another case, after the 2016 election, some of her students were nervous about the possible ramifications of the president's rhetoric regarding refugees, especially those from certain countries. This was a common situation throughout the country at the time, when students (and teachers) expressed concern about their place and safety in society. Emily narrates how she felt that she was proactive by letting the students' families know about their rights:

And so this I sent out a letter to the parents about the Safe Schools Act so they knew that ICE can never enter a school, that we can never give information and I was told by my district—by one person in my district—that I was being too political. So that's one of the hard things, convincing them that there is a difference between being political and caring and being empathetic and giving facts they deserve to have. And also making sure that our teachers know that if they are approached by ICE they can never open their mouth about it. So that kind of stuff gets frustrating.

Emily faced isolation and limited feedback from school administration, highlighting the need for cultural brokers to bridge communication between families and schools. Emily sent the letter to parents about the Safe Schools Act, ensuring confidentiality and safety for students from immigrant backgrounds. However, she was criticized for being too political, while Emily saw it as a solution to a potential problem.

Emily chose to become part of the school's student assistance program (SAP) to ensure that her students weren't falling through the cracks as she says "it's so easy to overlook what's going with the ESL kids" who may not be used to the system and don't know who to go to for help. However, she "had a close relationship with [her] kids because [she] had them year after year, that a lot of times I get what's not going to be shared in other classrooms."

She especially noted that many of her students arrive with trauma from being uprooted or experiencing homelessness or, in some cases, extreme violence. Joining the SAP allowed her to take action in order to be an effective teacher of students from refugee backgrounds.

In another case, Emily once contacted a family directly to explain an American cultural norm, the breaking of which would potentially prompt a visit from youth protective services. She acknowledged that she potentially broke school codes and rules and that "Some of the legal stuff is very difficult for me to deal with." Emily adds, "I'm struggling a little bit with that, of knowing where do I draw the line, what is on paper is the right thing to do versus what I know my families need."

She was warned by her administration to abide by school code rules and "not cross the line again." But she relates her frustration with the status quo and tries to consider new ways to address issues that arise:

> I don't know if it's just because of this year, or because now I'm five years into doing this and I'm starting to see the same patterns emerge.... I'm part of the Student Assistance Team and in a normal case we would have called [youth protective services] and gotten them involved. But because it was a cultural thing, I really felt we kind of needed to go through some back doors. And I'm not opposed to calling [youth protective services] if it continues, but I felt like education more essential in this case than punitive or perceived punitive....

They're trying to do what's best but they usually roll up with a cuff and it's not a good situation.. . . the family was somewhat receptive. I mean, they were clearly disturbed that we did it, but I feel like it went as well as one could expect.

The pandemic posed even more challenges for students from refugee backgrounds. Emily shared that, during the COVID-19 pandemic, emotional, academic, social, and cultural pressures for students increased exponentially. These challenges were compounded by language barriers, parents who may not have attended school, and the need to recreate school at home for their children. This was especially challenging for older students, who may have had responsibilities at home like caring for younger family members or finding a job.

During the COVID-19 pandemic, English-language learners faced a multiplicity of equity disparities, and many families were disconnected from the outside world. Emily said, "I have a handful of kids who are fully online because their parents are absolutely terrified . . . [in] one of my families, the children have not stepped foot outside of their house since March." But she saw an alarming "difference in their personalities" and that "all the brightness has gone out of their eyes. They're so timid."

Fearing for their children's lives, parents kept them indoors, causing anxiety and social separation. Emily expressed her wish to help these families understand scientific facts about COVID-19, because some families were not connected or informed. However, the pandemic also allowed some positive growth. For instance, access to technology increased, as did student autonomy. Emily shared that, after the pandemic, teachers saw a boost in students' self-advocacy and communication with teachers. She said, "For some, [the pandemic is] an opportunity to collaborate in different ways."

Students learned to email teachers for questions, providing a sense of self-advocacy. Distance communication provided anonymity, making some students feel more comfortable discussing fears, insecurities, and happiness. Emily felt a growth in "familial relationship with [her] students." Like Emily, Nicole also demonstrated vulnerability and ability to overcome challenges in her role in different ways. The next section will discuss these themes in her story. See box 5.2 for Nicole's found poem.

NICOLE'S STORY

Nicole's found poem presents her as a thirty-eight-year-old, middle-class, White woman who has been a K–12 ESL teacher for fifteen years. She also has a background in elementary and special education, with her undergraduate preparation in an urban educational setting. She has a master of arts

Nicole

"I am an expert in my field!"/A (bit vocal) thirty-eight middle-class, Caucasian, female K–12 ESL teacher./Social Work, special . . . elementary . . . and urban education background./Master's degree./First in family! A huge accomplishment!/Catholic but agnostic. Spiritual . . . oriented around family./Mom . . . a beacon of light and a symbol of strength for a female./I am honored./My niche, my specialty, my children. I'm like their second mom,/Many hats. ESL teacher, social worker, school counselor, and parent!/It was good. A strength and a challenge/

I learned so much from them when I taught high school./We could teach and learn./Philosophical and political . . . /views not in the best interest of English learners./"You have to build trust, and I feel like it takes time."/What's going on?/I was just a person to help bridge the conversation between the administration and kids./There are days that I feel like we don't get much done academically, but it's okay.

degree in reading education, which she describes as a "huge accomplishment" and which she also says has allowed her to teach K–12.

Her experience includes social work, specifically working with kids with autism and developmental delays in multiple inner-city and suburban districts. Nicole currently works as an ESL teacher that gets placed in different schools through a county-run educational unit to support the needs of multilingual learners; therefore, she has had experience in many different contexts, often changing schools she supports every year. As in Emily's experience, in Nicole's experience, the demographics of students she has taught has fluctuated in the years she has been a teacher, such that she has "taught kids from all over the world," including, especially in the past five years, students who are refugees.

She sees her experience in working with different schools and exceptional students, with distinct needs, as helping to prepare her for working with students who come from refugee backgrounds and who "do come with trauma and . . . have emotional challenges." As she states, "kids that have trauma cannot learn until they feel safe, until they feel cared for. Until they feel that, they're not going to be able to retain academics."

She feels that, as the ESL teacher, she had multiple roles. As she explains, "I was also the social worker, the school counselor. I was the parent, I was . . . you know I wore many hats." With the "influx in children who are refugees," Nicole related that she became like a "second mom" to her students. What do mothers do in Nicole's world? Just like her own mother, Nicole became "a symbol of strength," to support "her kids."

Nicole is an "agnostic" who practices the "golden rule," treating others as you want to be treated and placing yourself in others' shoes. Her strengths include empathy, learning compassion at home, being a lifelong learner, and practicing role reversal. She says of her students, "Once I get to know them, I just think about my own family and how I would want it if the roles were reversed.... You know, would there be people available to help my family or myself get through the school system that's totally foreign to?"

VULNERABILITY IN NICOLE'S STORY

While Nicole calls the education of refugee students as sort of her "niche" or "specialty," she acknowledges that "I feel there's a high need for getting better. For districts and schools to get better and provide services to them, not just language, but otherwise, other services that are available to them that maybe they don't know." Because of Nicole's role as an ESL teacher who gets placed in different schools depending on local needs, she has had a unique view of the needs of schools—and the need for herself to continuously learn. As a lifelong learner, Nicole has had to make constant adjustments to her curriculum and perspectives as her schools and backgrounds of students change.

For instance, in the following excerpt, Nicole narrates the difficulties and discomforts that come with not knowing, or being uncertain about, how to best meet the needs of her students:

> I think it's a limitation for me personally, because I ... I know only so much ... I've been at this school for two years now, so this family arrived though probably four years ago. For me, I mean, these boys, the two that I have currently, do suffer from trauma, even the parents too. I know that they ... they share snippets with me but I don't know their full, full background, and I don't expect to, and I'm okay with that. It's up to them if they want to share that but it's hard sometimes to navigate that sometimes or figure out ways. I mean, we have a counselor at school who is great and everything, and I do think my boys see her once a week or talk with her once a week, or at least the oldest one, but I don't know. For example, this week or two weeks ago actually, the oldest one shared this with me, and I was appreciative he shared this with me, and he didn't want his mom to know though that he was sharing this with me, so it put me in a really hard predicament.

Not only does Nicole have to learn how to work with the counselor in this situation to help her understand the needs of students who have experienced trauma, but she also has to navigate different cultural expectations—understanding how to understand the boys' feelings while also respecting the views of the parents.

Nicole discussed her position of being vulnerable, or being the unknowing or uncomfortable party, through her discussion of learning about the Muslim culture of many of her students. She discusses that sometimes her lack of knowledge caused her some discomfort, but working through that discomfort allowed her to be a better teacher. She describes this experience:

> I mean you, I feel like it just, you just learn as you know your students. You know now, when I work with my Arabic speakers, because of my experience in [name of school] . . . they taught me so much about the Muslim culture, of how different parts of Syria and even part of like the Middle East . . . I learned so much from them when I taught high school. They would share things with me that I was astounded to hear, that I was so naive to not think happened, but it really does happen, and not until I taught high school did I truly realize, oh my gosh, this stuff is really happening. Just walking down the street, a lot of my Muslim families . . . they shared so much with me that I was just astounded by them. Just walking down the street, our girls . . . I had a non-Muslim student touch one of our girl's hijab and they just did not understand how disrespectful that is.

She describes the incident in this way: "It was such a memorable moment for me in learning about them, religiously and just in general." Because she was able to learn more about their lives, she was able to be a more effective teacher. However, initially, she had to accept that she did not know what experiences they had, and she had to be willing to acknowledge that she had much to learn—and co-learn—from them. Her remark about these occasions highlights Nicole's joys and delights in learning about something that initially made her the uncomfortable party: "So it was really a wonderful learning experience but a challenge at the same time."

Nicole also points to vulnerability that can emerge from lack of preparation. She emphasizes that her various experiences have prepared her well for her current role:

> I feel like . . . being that I have worked with children who have challenges behaviorally, challenges emotionally. That has helped me build up stamina to think on my feet quicker whereas other teachers who may not have that background might feel overwhelmed and kind of shut down . . . because . . . you know, public education can be challenging, especially for new teachers. And I feel like because of my background experiences and being that my undergrad was in urban education, my student teaching, all my very beginning experiences were in locations where there was a higher challenge or a higher need I should say, you know.. . . There's so many layers of school success.

Nicole proposes that, without all the experiences, teachers in general, herself included, would not be well prepared for the rigors of supporting students from refugee backgrounds. Nicole demonstrates the realization that learning to teach is a lifelong process; that teachers have to acknowledge what they don't know and what they need to learn; and that teachers have to be comfortable with uncertainty.

OVERCOMING CHALLENGES IN NICOLE'S STORY

Throughout her narratives, Nicole highlights her challenges as an ESL teacher who advocates for refugee students and families. She struggled with limited resources and leadership that had contradictory beliefs about education of multilingual learners. She shares that, in high-achieving districts, school administration, teachers, and decision-makers often have unrealistic expectations of ESL children. Nicole stresses that "other content area teachers aren't always abreast of best practices regarding language learners."

For instance, Nicole discusses how she overcame a challenge with her new administration and their conflicting ideas about how to best serve multilingual students, many of whom were from refugee backgrounds. She expresses frustration with district standards requiring ESL students to complete reading tasks without providing the necessary time and tools for differentiation according to students' diverse needs. She narrates this issue:

> Another challenge . . . the school district I mentioned is very rigorous. You know they have very high standards and I respect that but I also, we also need to be realistic and what demands we're placing on our English learners. So they read novels in fifth grade. They read eight novels in a school year. I have never heard of this in my life. So my principal asked me, she said, "Nicole, I really want you to do novels with fifth grade." And I said, "okay," I said, "well" . . . but she didn't tell me how many or anything, it was just like okay, I'm thinking like one, maybe two per year. Oh no. So when my boss, I have a curriculum that I'm supposed to implement from the [county-based unit] that is a language curriculum through National Geographic. It is made for English learners. While my principal does not respect this curriculum, she thinks it's too easy. It's not rigorous enough, she thinks it's discriminatory because she doesn't believe that English learners should be getting separate instruction in a small-group setting. But when they get English services, they come for a small group. So there's a very big philosophical difference with her personally and I've never had a principal like her in my life. So it's been a bit of a challenge because her own philosophical and political views are things that she wants to change in her building yet they're not in the best interest of English learners. It's not what is

best practice for English learners so I've been, I've had to challenge her a lot this year and it's been a bit exhausting.

In her story, she discusses how she felt that her principal was not following the rules for how to provide the allotted hours for ESL students required by law. The administrator considered ESL pullout to be discriminatory, while Nicole considered it to be their civil right and an effective way that students would learn.

Eventually, Nicole's director had to intervene with the principal and come to an agreement about how to provide services in the building. Ultimately, after a year of working with the administrator, Nicole came to see her point of view; however, she still held on to her beliefs about the best way to provide instruction to her students. "Getting to know her more, I now understand more where she's coming from when she said that because I can see in so many ways, and it took me a whole year." Nicole narrates her efforts:

> I'm doing my best to work through, I feel like it is a good thing that I am where I am this year though because I think without my presence there, our kids maybe would have been slighted. I think our ELs would have not been able to get as many services as they deserve. Because I know my job and I know how to fight for you know, based on the state regs.

This situation demonstrates Nicole's willingness to take risks to advocate for her students. Because she faced a challenging situation, which she claimed she had never experienced before, she was forced into taking steps that were perhaps anxiety-induced, especially since she had to oppose her principal. She worked confidently, though, within the current system to overcome this issue. She showed a readiness to consider new ways of connecting with leadership to advocate for her students from refugee backgrounds.

Nicole also identifies mental-health support as the greatest need of her students and reiterated the need for more training in "trauma-informed education . . . social-emotional learning . . . [and] training for stamina" to sustain the prolonged physical and mental effort required of teachers. She explains, "These kids are stressed out because of their mental health, emotional . . . and behavior challenges . . . intermixed with learning a new language . . . and trying to fit in with a whole new culture and environment." As their teacher, she needs time to differentiate instructions and build a trusting relationship with her students and their families.

Nicole's approach to helping her students is first to acknowledge that she may not understand their situations and has to co-learn with them, as was discussed with regard to Nicole's vulnerability. But leaning into that vulnerability to try to understand their experiences and situations allows her to devise new strategies based on innovative thoughts and actions. Nicole tries to build empathy by learning their stories and trying to place herself in their shoes.

In the previous section on vulnerability, Nicole discussed her co-learning with her Muslim students. She summarizes her two years working at that school as a "strength" and a "challenge." She relates that experience:

> The last two years at [name of school] that was a strength and a challenge that I had dealt with there. It was the kids' strength but also a challenge with them because sometimes there would be tension and we had to work closely with the social workers to fizzle that . . . my kids asked me, "Ms. N, can we have a space for prayer during the school day?" And I said, "Well, let's talk about that some more, let's talk to the administration." So they were on board and they said sure.

Ultimately, by showing her vulnerability and readiness to understand her students and their position, she learned about the possibilities that were in place to help support her students. Nicole's focus on not just academic development but also on the necessary socioemotional elements to her students' learning spurred her on to engage in new ways of thinking and action to promote effective learning.

Nicole also points out various changes due to the pandemic that actually helped in some ways, as in Emily's experience. Nicole narrates that the COVID-19 pandemic "changed all of us . . . everyone has grown so much exponentially in so many different ways in reaching all of our kids." She emphasizes how the innovative ways all teachers had to engage in to communicate with, connect with, and teach their students built new pathways of communication. Through technology, they built "intimate personal connections" multiple times a day. She adds, "They trusted me and relied on me." Nicole expands on this notion of innovative and changing communication patterns and shares how her relationship with her students and their families developed more during the pandemic:

> Yes. I mean, it's always a challenge, pre-pandemic, to provide enough interpretation and translation to our families, but I feel like with this pandemic, that is something . . . I felt like I was successful with that prior pandemic, but I feel like, now, it's just . . . It's extra especially with my family too or from refugee backgrounds, it's so personal with them. It's like a different level of interaction. It's daily. I mean, multiple times a day. Those parents and I are so close now, not that we weren't before, but . . . They trusted me and relied on me. We depend on each other for communication, but then I can't even tell you the hundreds and hundreds of messages that were relayed just since in the last year. I mean, my normal communication log that I keep is typically ten to twelve pages for a whole school year, I'm already at twelve pages and we're halfway through. Do you know what I mean? I always call them. Because of that, the level of

trust that I have with my families is very high. I mean, they just are so thankful, and they just trust me with their children. It's a very big honor, and it's a whole other level of intimate personal connection than I've ever experienced before the pandemic.

Students emailed her all the time, asking questions and sharing daily stories. Also, collaboration between parents and children's teachers shifted significantly. Communication became more frequent, with parents and teachers connecting multiple times daily.

In Nicole's narrative, being isolated during periods of social distancing made school community members appreciate one another. It brought all of them closer together in the face of adversity. Nicole says of her principal in the school, that it took some time, and perseverance, to learn to appreciate each other's strengths. Nicole described that, after working together for a year and traveling through the pandemic together, "We understand each other and work better now together. I know she cares about our kids; she fights for them!" Despite their differences in approach to their care and advocacy for students, Nicole and her principal ultimately came to understand those differences and appreciate each other's style.

REFLECTION

Both teachers, Emily and Nicole, have years of direct work experience with students from refugees and displaced backgrounds. They, each through her own lens, share similar ideas of what is important in the education of refugee and displaced students. These lenses were formed through their personal and professional experiences. While Emily has taught as the ESL specialist at one school for a number of years, Nicole has moved around as part of her job as an ESL teacher that supports different schools, perhaps changing each year.

Through their narratives, both teachers show aspects of vulnerability at times alongside strategies to overcome the challenges presented. They both demonstrated that they experienced discomfort with being the unknowing and felt the tension with realization that they often did not know what to do in varying situations. However, they work through these vulnerabilities to find creative, risk-taking, and innovative ways to tackle challenges. Often these ways provided some anxiety along the way, but they were able to find the joys and delights in ultimately supporting their students.

They both, however, identify several factors that hinder providing a just, safe learning atmosphere. In their opinion, to successfully prepare this student population for the future, teachers need more time, specialized prior preparation, practical professional development, and more freedom and teacher empowerment. Both participants' insights revealed a need for more time. They struggle with dividing their time to include all the required regular classroom activities, teach the English-language development curriculum, and differentiate instruction according to students' linguistic abilities.

They need time to focus on teaching, rebuild the students' academic foundation, and establish a trusting relationship with students and families. Additionally, teachers need time to work together and collaborate. Emily and Nicole also called for practical and adequate preparation of teachers to establish a strong foundation for the classroom and eliminate faulty structures in school entities. There was a clear urgency in the teachers' voices, highlighting the need for better preparation of ESL-certified and other educators who play a role in the education of refugee and displaced students.

This training should include trauma-informed, social-emotional teaching and learning. Nicole's experience, for example, suggests that there should be training and practice in teaching skills in different districts in varying contexts. Emily's experience "flying blind" despite earning an ESL certificate suggests that there should be expanded training beyond minimal requirements.

Nicole believes her special-education background and social-work experience make her well suited for teaching students of refugee and displaced backgrounds. She calls for better preparation for all teachers, emphasizing trauma-informed education, social-emotional learning, and training for stamina. She also emphasizes the need for informed public education, urban-school training, and robust professional development and training to create knowledgeable teachers who understand the academic and nonacademic needs of students.

As Nicole did, Emily experienced professional isolation and frustration with top-down leadership and decision-making practices in which teachers are not invited to participate. These decisions prioritized high-stakes testing, conformed with cookie-cutter standards, and forced assessment-driven curricula on their teachers and students. In her narrative, Emily said, "We don't get feedback from anybody else unless it's the principal who stops in for fifteen or twenty minutes . . . my opinion isn't worth very much." This prompted her to join specific groups to solicit feedback and discuss best practices, in addition to getting to know her students.

Research suggests that robust education systems recognize that school events are influenced by society and that a healthy system requires interconnected institutions to support all stakeholders. Prioritizing vulnerable children and strengthening global emergency preparedness and response plans are crucial. Stakeholders should coordinate efforts across humanitarian sectors, including child welfare, youth development, and education sectors, to serve all students.

Emily and Nicole emphasize the need for teachers to work closely with students of refugee and displaced backgrounds and their families to understand how to support them effectively. Family social capital, such as technical skills and parents' connections, increased student engagement in learning. Multiple platforms should be used to communicate information, particularly in native languages.

In particular, both narrate experiences where mental-health support and family engagement were crucial for their students' well-being; achieving such support and engagement required close coordination with school professionals and families. Nicole focused on building connection and trust between them so that they see Nicole as an ally. Emily emphasized that their rights and responsibilities within the school and larger community were paramount and that teachers should be willing to go against popular opinion (or even school regulations) to ensure them.

REFERENCES

Beghetto, R. A. (2021). How times of crisis serve as a catalyst for creative action: An agentic perspective. *Frontiers in Psychology*, *11*, 600685.

Brantmeier, E. J. (2013). Pedagogy of vulnerability: Definitions, assumptions, and applications. In J. Lin, R. Oxford, & E. J. Brantmeier (Eds.), *Re-envisioning higher education: Embodied pathways to wisdom and transformation* (pp. 95–106). Information Age Publishing.

Brunila, K., & Rossi, L.-M. (2018). Identity politics, the ethos of vulnerability, and education. *Educational Philosophy and Theory*, *50*(3), 287–98. https://doi.org/10.1080/00131857.2017.1343115.

Cohen, A. K., & Cromwell, J. R. (2021). How to respond to the COVID-19 pandemic with more creativity and innovation. *Population Health Management*, *24*(2), 153–55.

Dale, M., & Frye, E. M. (2009). Vulnerability and love of learning as necessities for wise teacher education. *Journal of Teacher Education*, *60*(2), 123–30.

Dyer, C. (2023). The Role of Vulnerability in Building Trust and Creating a Positive Work Environment. https://tinyurl.com/e52x4ya4.

Gibson, C. B., & Manuel, J. A. (2003). Building trust. *Virtual teams that work*, 59–86.

Walters, H. (2012). Vulnerability is the birthplace of innovation, creativity and change: Brené Brown at TED2012. *https://blog.ted.com/vulnerability-is-the-birthplace-of-innovation-creativity-and-change-brene-brown-at-ted2012/comment-page-2/*, 19.

Watson, A., Lupton, D., & Michael, M. (2021). Enacting intimacy and sociality at a distance in the COVID-19 crisis: The sociomaterialities of home-based communication technologies. *Media International Australia*, *178*(1), 136–50. https://doi.org/10.1177/1329878X20961.

Chapter 6

Building Classroom Community and Advocacy

In this chapter, the authors explore classroom community building and advocacy in the narratives of two public-school teachers, Kay and Janet. Kay is a retired, suburban, elementary music teacher while Janet is a veteran teacher of English language arts in an urban high school. The authors argue that Kay and Janet are "equity-literate" (Gorski & Swalwell, 2015) educators of refugee students and that their stories demonstrate unique approaches to community building and advocacy in and out of the classroom. In the following sections, the authors will define community building and advocacy before moving on to demonstrate them in the narratives.

COMMUNITY BUILDING

Teacher education is rife with admonitions for teachers to build community in their classrooms. Preservice teachers learn to start class with icebreakers, practice routines, and co-construction of classroom norms. However, community building can be romanticized and assumed to be a by-product of a well-run classroom. Too often, new teachers experience a kind of professional culture shock in their new classrooms. They expect children will automatically reciprocate their goodwill and intentions as they diligently implement classroom management and lesson plans that center community building and an ethic of caring (Noddings, 1984).

Roxas (2011) aptly addresses how this is compounded in teachers' work with refugee students:

> Public school teachers are expected by the public to build communities in their classrooms. In addition to teaching academic core subjects, teachers are supposed to be teaching their students how to live in society, how to be supportive

of each other, and how to prepare themselves to be productive and cooperative members of the communities in which they live. However, these idyllic goals become complicated when we consider the sociopolitical and sociocultural contexts for refugee children who enter public schools today. Students will not automatically buy into the importance of building community in their classrooms if they have always been marginalized by members of the communities in which they live (p. 7).

What teachers learn in practice, although they may study it in theory, is that culturally relevant teachers (those who effectively build communities of learning in diverse classrooms) are socially and politically aware of the contexts of their students' lives and know how to incorporate this awareness into the curriculum (Ladson-Billings, 2006). Community building cannot be divorced from curriculum building and, as Roxas affirms, is a complicated endeavor in today's diverse classrooms. Further, classroom communities must be imagined as microcosms of the larger sociopolitical contexts of teachers and students' lives.

Definitions of community are deceptively simple yet vary widely. Even when this term is generally defined as a group of people who have something in common, one can easily become entangled in the myriad number of spaces, objects, and ideas that "something" might represent. Two distinct conceptions of community in Kay and Janet's narratives will be examined in this chapter: community-as-place and feeling of belonging.

Community-as-place answers the question, "Where are you from?" For refugee children, the "quest for a place to call home is central as they journey across geographical spaces . . . where [they also] need to create new, often temporary, social worlds and relationships" (Kohli, 2011, p. 313). Home is, on one level, a physical space; however, it is also a psychological, emotional, and social space. Both Kay and Janet talk about the "locational ties" (McIntyre & Abrams, 2021, p. 81) that shape their identities and, importantly, how these position them vis-a-vis their students.

Feeling of belonging, conceived of here as a social process realized when people come together through shared relational ties and values, is crucial for well-being (McIntyre & Abrams, 2021). Kohli (2011) describes refugee childrens' movements along three "tracks," including "the search for safety, *the growth of belonging*, and the will to succeed within new environments" (p. 313, italics added). Fostering growth of belonging in schools is necessary to develop the positive self-worth and positive relationships that promote learning.

Positive self-worth can be fostered when educators embrace notions of community cultural capital, or the knowledge, skills, abilities, and networks that students bring to school (Yosso, 2005). Schools that value and draw upon families' aspirational, linguistic, familial, social, navigational, and resistant capital are able to "transform education" by utilizing "assets that are already abundant" in students and their families' communities (p. 82). The larger purpose of struggling toward social justice, rather than co-opting or exploiting community capital, can thus be realized as teachers work to build classroom communities.

ADVOCACY

Advocacy generally means supporting a cause, promoting interests, or pleading for others. Kay and Janet, however, both stress the importance of *action* in advocating for their students. They recognize that knowing and doing are two different things. As Gorski and Swalwell (2023) affirm, if building social-justice awareness does not include taking action, it can be seen as a form of entitlement. These authors offer the equity-literacy framework as a way to help teachers avoid the trap of being stuck in a place of entitlement.

Equity literacy supports educators in creating and sustaining equitable schools. An equity-literate educator possesses the ability to recognize, respond, redress, actively cultivate, and sustain equity and justice (Gorski & Swalwell, 2015). Cultivating and sustaining equity and justice require advocacy rooted in action.

Further, action must move toward transformation of institutional policies and practices that filter down into the everyday experiences of students currently experiencing inequities. Without action, advocates may remain stuck in a never-ending time loop, pleading for the cause of another. Nontransformative advocacy, often carried out by "lone hero" teachers in classrooms, year after year, is an exhausting enterprise (Barret, Ford, & James, 2010).

As veteran teachers, both Kay and Janet share the unique rewards and challenges of this work. The remainder of the chapter will focus on Kay and Janet's stories of building community and advocating for refugee students. For Kay, advocacy for a just curriculum spurs a political career postretirement. See box 6.1 for Kay's found poem. Through these words, we see Kay as an engaged former teacher and political activist who genuinely cares about, and acts toward, equity and justice for refugee students and their families in her community.

KAY'S STORY

Kay describes herself as the youngest of seven children raised in a small town in the rural Midwest. Although her father served in the Navy, he left

> **Kay**
>
> A Euro-American (mainly German) woman/Who grew up in a small town,/The youngest of seven children.//From a family of/Open-minded travelers/With dreams.//A teacher-politician-woman-activist/Retired after more than twenty-five years of teaching children about music/And asking "What does this mean, and how does it relate to civil justice?"//Now running for political office,/Because it's time for women to be candidates!/Belonging to an interfaith group—preachers to politicians.//
>
> Listening in mosques and churches to hear the pulse of the congregation./They ask, "What are the issues?/Is it homelessness? Affordable housing? Health care? Education?"//Charity versus social justice . . . / It's like this: If you have a headache, you take an aspirin./Well, that's charity. It keeps going.//What is causing this headache?/You go to a doctor./That is social justice./I need to find out what is causing the problem to fix it.

the military before she was born. She attributes her personal and professional values to her family's influence and their "open-minded[ness]." She credits his service for his love of travel, something that Kay believes she learned from him.

Kay prefers the term "Euro-American" over White and describes her German ethnic heritage as central to her identity. Racially, Kay's identity mirrors that of eighty percent of the US teaching force (COE, 2023). It is important to consider teachers' and students' racial identities because incongruence has long been recognized as an issue that negatively affects student outcomes.

Kay taught for more than thirty years before retiring and running for a state-level political office. She spent the last twenty-five of those years in the same public elementary school. As Kay describes, her school experienced two major demographic shifts. First, in the 1990s, students and their families moved from two large urban centers in the upper Midwest to her school district. This shift was her first experience of demographic change. The school transitioned from enrolling predominantly White students to one that enrolled higher numbers of non-White students. The size of the school almost doubled at the same time.

Over the next decade, according to Kay, the community experienced another demographic shift. Black students with refugee backgrounds from Somalia and Sudan began to be enrolled. The decade of the 2010s saw further growth in racial, ethnic, linguistic, and religious diversity and in the student population overall. Kay's thinking and teaching shifted to reflect her students' lives and experiences.

Kay leads an engaged political career postretirement. She is an outspoken advocate of justice and equity through involvement with an organization that call itself a "multi-racial, state-wide, nonpartisan coalition of faith communities fighting for racial and economic justice in [state]" (reference omitted). Her political agenda stems from her teaching experiences across three decades.

COMMUNITY BUILDING IN KAY'S NARRATIVES

Community building in Kay's classroom was an active and complex process. It was rooted in her identity and experiences and evolved in response to shifting demographics. Her conceptions of community stem from her understanding of herself and her place in a large, rural household growing up with her family. Kay credits these relational and "locational ties" (McIntyre & Abrams, 2021, p. 81) for her values and beliefs.

She describes her family as open-minded travelers who taught her to value diversity. Although she "lived in [midwestern state] [her] whole life [and] grew up in a small town," she attributes these influences to have "come from all the older siblings and [her] parents." They were supportive in terms of education (only two of her siblings did not attend college), travel, and teaching. According to Kay, "There was that expansion—you go out. You go out. You see the world."

She says of herself, "I've always felt very strong that as an educator, my job is to show all the possibilities. Not [to] show my opinion or my preference for something, but to . . . show truth and honesty, rather than pretending it's not existing. [When I don't know something, it's important] to be honest about it and do a study of it." This determination to recognize and respond to her own limited knowledge is an important part of equity literacy (Gorski & Swalwell, 2015).

Kay also recognizes her church and the ethos of the 1970s as influencing her identity, values, and aspirations. She admires "three powerful women in her church" who were "intelligent, confident making decisions, speaking up in groups, and leading." She adds, "And so that was not abnormal for me—to see women being strong and leading and being vocal."

The church, according to Kay, also taught her to ask, "What does this mean, and how does it relate to civil justice?" She shares her belief through the following analogy:

You're by a river, and there are people coming down the river that need to be saved and you are pulling them out. One by one. You pull them out one by one. One by one. And then you go, "But what's happening up the river that's causing them to be in the river?" And that's social justice. That's the social justice question.

Kay claims that the state university she attended gave her a "broader view of music and the world." Moving away from her home and family, she quickly developed a sense of belonging in college as a musician. The music program she chose felt like the perfect fit. She describes it as eclectic and diverse. She enjoyed the experimental approach that "helped give [her] a broader view of culture and the world."

During Kay's career, demographic shifts transformed her classroom. Kay describes her school as being initially "homogeneous" and notes that socioeconomic backgrounds represented the "only diversity." As she describes the first major shift, she references racial identifiers and locational ties of her new students. These are related to "family situations" and "behaviors" associated with "poverty" that necessitated, in Kay's words, professional development to help mitigate the "culture shock" experienced by the teachers:

> And then the first migration started in the '90s when families started to migrate from Detroit and Chicago. That was a culture shock for the school. The school went from about five hundred students to nine hundred, and we had to suddenly figure out how to teach children of color . . . what those family situations were like and behaviors and how to work with all of that. We had some really good workshops on teaching people in poverty.

Like her peers, Kay was born, grew up, attended college, and lived in racially segregated spaces. Like most White teachers, her experiences working with non-White students were limited. Further, her perspectives were shaped by popular professional-development programs aimed at White teachers, which reinforced deficit perspectives and negative stereotypes.

Kay reports that she began to develop more culturally relevant (Ladson-Billings, 2006) pedagogical skills. She changed her music curriculum to draw upon the strengths of her new students. She worked diligently to build bridges between their lives and school. She reports that she was not well supported in this endeavor, remembering that she "had to do more with that [her]self."

A decade later, Kay's school experienced another significant shift in demographics. As Kay describes, "And then in the early 2000s, we started to see another change in student population from immigrants and refugees from Somalia." There is a notable widening arc of discomfort as she describes how she was challenged by curricular boundaries in unexpected ways:

> [At first,] I didn't see a large effect on what was happening to the curriculum. I was supported well by the EL teachers. But as the population increased into the next decade, 2010s, there was quite a big population then of students from Somalia and students also from Sudan. But what I discovered from the students whose families were from Somalia, for these conservative Muslims, music was against their religion. So that was a conflict. And I'm sure [students] were struggling.

Building community in her classroom felt like an almost impossible task. She knew children struggled to integrate the social and cultural norms of their new schooling with those at home:

> And then coming to school, I'm asking them to sing [in mixed-gender classrooms]. I'm asking them to play instruments. And of course, some children are like, "Oh yeah, I love it." And then some students would say, "Well, I can't do music." And as the classes grew from twenty-five percent to forty percent Muslim, a lot of the children didn't want to sing or were confused about whether they could sing. Parents didn't come to concerts because that was a really new thing. So yeah, it was a little tough. That was frustrating.

Community is centered in relationships. Relationships with parents are key to developing strong classroom communities. The ethnic, linguistic, and religious differences between school culture and norms and her students' families severely impacted Kay's ability to build community in her classroom. Caught between the demands of school policies (music is a required class for all students) and the requests of religiously conservative parents that their children not sing in mixed-gender groups or, in some cases, at all, Kay describes her classroom as a "battle[ground]."

ADVOCACY IN KAY'S NARRATIVES

Kay also felt limited in her ability to develop culturally relevant curricula for her Muslim students. She reports, "So I tried to look up on the internet—Somali music. And a lot of it was sacred. And the public school has a hands off with sacred. So there's a fine line to walk with that." Language was another barrier. Even when she was able to talk with parents, she remembers that "most of the parents were wanting to get their child out of music class." At this point in her career, Kay recognized that a lack of resources for teachers contributes to the "lone hero" (Barret, Ford, & James, 2010) approach that many teachers take.

Kay began to take on a more active role in advocating for curricular shifts. As she describes it from her current vantage point, her students' families are a source of strength. She says, "[My students'] greatest strength is commitment to family. They're coming together as a community, and they're helping each other out. I think that's a huge strength. Family and community. We take care of people. We need to relearn that here."

Kay describes the evolution of her curriculum in stages led by negotiations with families that she characterizes as finding "common ground." She remembers, "Many of the parents seemed to be okay with instruments and drums. So that was the first step. That's some common ground, and we can start with that." She recalls how interacting with cultural navigators was key for her pedagogical development. One cultural navigator introduced her to the Somali national anthem.

Kay recalls how this affected her emotionally: "And as he is playing it for me, he's getting teary eyed and choked up. He grew up with it. He is so sad. He's no longer able to be in Somalia because of the wars." For Kay, there was a sense of urgency and solidarity. She moved beyond being the "lone hero" (Barret, Ford, & James 2010) in a battle with curriculum, students, and parents.

She began to draw upon community resources to shape a curriculum that would strengthen her classroom community in new ways. The following story ends with a parent, tears in his eyes, telling Kay, "Oh, you are including us. You are showing that part." As Kay remembers, "Yes, he was very, very heartened by it."

> So I used [the patriotic Somali songs] in a unit. There's all of these beautiful celebrations of so many different cultural things. And so we had a day where we talked about Eid and about the families coming together and the prayers and the gift-giving . . . those things that are common. Then we talked about the prayers and facing Mecca. And, fortunately, about that time, there was a young Somali rap artist who came out with a tune, and it was used in the World Cup. So I used that video. That really helped the students feel special, feel connected to this, "Oh, this is what we celebrate. You're asking everybody in the classroom to understand what we celebrate and why we celebrate it and how we celebrate it." I invited students to share stories of their families celebrating. I incorporated dances and songs with instruments and historical pieces and customs. In so many of these, there's candles, there's family, there's giving, there's prayer, there's all of these pieces that are similar. Quite honestly, Advent was the last one I added to that unit because I was nervous. I taught during the years where you don't celebrate Christmas in the schools. I thought, "Oh, but why? I'm teaching about every other religion and culture. I need to also be comfortable teaching about Advent and Santa." So that was my unit in December, and I liked it.

After retiring, Kay campaigned for a state-level political office representing the district in which she taught and lives. She attributes a new perspective to her work with Somali community members. The Somali community members she mentions in her teaching stories are parents and cultural navigators who, she says now, don't represent all of Somali culture but a particular conservative branch that follows "a few imams." More complex and nuanced perspectives about Somali culture and Muslim religion emerge across the interviews while Kay campaigns for office.

Political involvement has given Kay a different role from which to experience refugee students and families. She states that it was a lack of time, too many students, and curricular restrictions that kept her too busy and just trying to get by as a classroom teacher—that she didn't have the space or time to reflect. She wishes now that she "could have done more with" Somali music in her classroom.

She still wishes she "would've been able to make those connections when [she] was teaching because the wealth is there and the music is there." As a political advocate, Kay realizes that "to change a policy, you have to work with whatever politician is in office." She recounts meetings with local and state-level officials. She credits her ability to be "nonpartisan" with enabling her to work back and forth between her communities and governmental institutions.

For Kay, over thirty years of teaching was not enough. She remains committed to equity and justice through her political career. When asked about the connection between her justice-oriented political advocacy and teaching, she cites curiosity as a key ingredient. She declares, "[I love] the social-justice piece and getting to know people from different faiths and different cultures. I enjoy mixing it up. I'm socializing with people and getting to know them. I'm curious about that."

Like Kay, Janet is a veteran teacher dedicated to her work with refugee communities. Her contexts, however, are quite different. See box 6.2 for Janet's found poem. Through these words, we see Janet as a critically conscious and overtly caring teacher who explicitly draws upon her own background and experiences to bridge the distance between her students' in- and out-of-school lives. Her nuanced understanding of her students' experiences is an incredible asset and, in her words, an "advantage" upon which she draws in her teaching.

JANET'S STORY

Janet describes herself through a complex network of identities. Race, ethnicity, political status, gender, religion, and language all provide intersectional perspectives that inform her life. Above all, she is a mother. As she states,

Janet

African American teacher-mother-researcher-immigrant-Christian-woman./Motherhood is the most important for me—/I have to make decisions,/It doesn't have a shelf life.//Over ten years teaching in an urban high school—/[Where] different parts of the world come together./I am an immigrant myself. (I'm not a refugee.)/I give them room to explore experiences.//English is an advantage./I navigate language and know—/Sometimes there is a reason behind/Why something is happening.//I switch the language/And ask them the same thing in Swahili./I wonder,/Just how much is lost for them in communication?//

Social Justice? I'm very interested in how people take up that term,/It's loaded and contentious./We all use it,/But we all have different meanings attached to it.//I know who I am doing it,/I'm aware of when I'm not doing it./The act of teaching students English—speaking English, writing English—/Is an act of activism and social justice.//Think like a parent./What would you want done/For your child/In a similar situation?//My job is not a chore./It's not a burden./It is something that I enjoy, something that I look forward to,/Interacting and exchanging ideas.

being a mother "doesn't have a shelf life" and involves the responsibility of decision-making. It is a central and stable part of her identity.

Janet is highly educated. She earned a Ph.D. in curriculum and instruction and a master's degree in TESL. She attended college in India. She has taught in the US public-school system for more than ten years. At the time of the interview, she had been at the same high school for seven years. She reports that her district is a refugee resettlement center for organizations like Catholic Charities. She describes the demographics of the school as constantly shifting, with groups of refugees and immigrants consistently arriving from various regions of the world.

Although she holds a TESL license, Janet teaches high-school juniors and seniors in a "regular" (i.e., not ESL) classroom where she teaches language arts, literature, and writing. Like all teachers in her building, Janet works extensively with students who have "just emerged" from direct ESL instruction. As many as eighty percent of her students in a single class might meet this criteria. With a critical consciousness informed by her life experiences, Janet deftly maneuvers teaching as in-the-moment opportunities (rather than as insurmountable challenges) with professional ease and expertise.

COMMUNITY BUILDING IN JANET'S NARRATIVES

Janet builds community by explicitly fostering a feeling of belonging based on "shared relational ties and values" (McIntyre & Abrams, 2021, p. 81). She works to build a classroom space where children feel welcome and safe. This pedagogical approach is important given that "the search for safety [and] the growth of belonging" are crucial to refugee childrens' wellbeing (Kohli, 2011, p. 313). She describes herself in this way: "I'm not a refugee, but I'm an immigrant. That experience of being an immigrant and knowing some of the things that I needed to navigate the system in a new country, that helps when I talk to the students."

Janet recognizes that belonging does not mean assimilation. She stresses the importance of her students' "need to remain true to who they are, to the way they were brought up, to what they know to be the essence of their life and worldview." She tells them that "knowing about where you live, how they do things, [and] what the expectations are does not diminish your own [self and culture]." She wants her students to "have their own identity" but also the "openness to learn new things." She advises them to "pick what you take, and leave what you don't need" when it comes to fitting in.

In building a community of belonging, Janet draws upon the metaphor of parenting. She asks, "What would you want done for your child in a similar situation?" She states, "Of course it [motherhood] finds its way into teaching, but putting motherhood at the forefront is about what I choose to take advantage of in life and what I choose to relegate to the sidelines for the time being." She adds, "You only have a limited time to be an active, hands-on type of parent and then the students leave the nest."

This last statement seems the most telling to the authors, who wonder if Janet meant "children leave the nest"; however, the use of "students," is fitting and aligns with Janet's narratives throughout the interviews. She describes herself as purposeful and holding high expectations:

> If I separate in my mind being a teacher and being a human in general, I would say that motherhood does not play such a big role in my teaching. It's more in my personal life and life choices. But then knowing what education can do, what doors education can open and how through my life experiences, then I know. Then that makes me more purposeful with my students and in my practice.

In her words, Janet thinks of teaching as "being a human in general" more than being a mother. Yet, she worries about her students and often does more than she is paid to do. Janet tells how she worried about a Swahili-speaking student who was sent to her room because she didn't know her bus number or where her stop was. After calling the girl's home, Janet was able to confirm the correct stop. An hour later, the uncle called Janet to let her know the girl had gotten off at the wrong stop, but she was safe at home.

As Janet describes her feelings about the event, she acknowledges that it made her "want to do more than [she is] paid to do." She says, "Thinking about all that, and worrying about the child, wondering what happened to her. And even if she did get lost, how will she be able to explain her circumstance to a stranger who would be wanting to help her? So, it's sad. So those kinds of things that make you want to do more than you're paid to do."

In another narrative, Janet talks about an ill child who was brought to the nurse and for whom Janet was asked to translate. According to Janet, "With COVID, there are so many rules and communicating at all using Google is impossibly difficult." Janet wondered if the child had a fever "because she was shaking. It was warmer, but then she was shivering and she didn't really have a sweater." Janet "facilitated the communication and then used [her] phone to call home." Janet continues the story:

> But then the girl was shivering and there was no blanket there. So, I always carry a shawl in my backpack because I get cold easily. So I went ahead and got my shawl from my backpack and gave it to her, and told her to go lie down, and when I hear from the mother, I will come get her. So, I remember that. So . . . it's one of those times where I mean, you think like a parent and what you would want done for your child if they were in a similar situation.

While the authors agree with Janet that these represent "being a [good] human in general," they also recognize the many ways that Janet goes above and beyond to help children in her school—in other words, she teaches as if students are *her own* children rather than "other people's children" (Delpit, 1995) for whom she might have limited responsibility. As a teacher, she "think[s] like a parent and what [she] would want done for [her] child." Janet knows that children need to "believe that they themselves are cared for and learn to care" if they are to succeed academically (Noddings, 1995, p. 675).

Fostering a feeling of belonging for oneself in the profession is as important as working to build it for one's students. Janet eloquently speaks of the rewards of her job:

> My job is not a chore. It's not a burden. It is something that I enjoy doing. It is something that I look forward to doing. I see it as interacting, exchanging ideas, and discussing things. Talking about things that I like. And since I teach language arts, and I've always liked reading and writing, it's just another opportunity for me to go and do something that I love. And I think having that kind of job really helps. Caring for people and about people, and being able to make a difference, especially in the lives of immigrants. Being able to make a difference

in their lives, and being able to say that I helped them along their life's journey. That is rewarding.

Clearly, Janet knows she is important in her students' lives. She stresses that the positive relationships she is able to build with students change everything. As she states, she can't meet all of her students' needs, but she "know[s] where to direct them" if she is "able to build positive relationships with them" and they "open up . . . and tell [her] what they need."

ADVOCACY IN JANET'S NARRATIVES

Janet does not see herself as a "lone hero" (Barret, Ford, & James, 2010). She describes the many roles that are assumed by adults in her school—from social workers to community-food-bank volunteers to counselors. She appreciates the opportunity to "have a professional community that is like-minded. Talking about those [social-justice and equity] issues and to each other about resources that we can use to enhance students' learning."

In addition to her own personal and professional experiences, Janet's dissertation project led her to reflect deeply on social justice and advocacy in her work. As she states, "Before getting into [my project], I was just teaching and giving students choices. But now when I do it, I know who I am doing it. I'm aware of when I'm not doing it. So it has made me very aware and attuned to my practice." As Ladson-Billings (2006) might agree, when Janet recognizes that her practice is as much about who she is as what she does (or does not do), then she is, indeed, attuned to practicing culturally relevant pedagogy.

Through her project, Janet came to realize that "sometimes [social justice] may mean small incremental changes." She urges teachers to "take matters into their own hands and effect change where you can." Even changes that are not "huge" or noticed by everyone will "make a difference." For Janet, small changes ripple out and may impact "a few students, the whole class, [her] entire practice, or the people that [she] collaborates with." She advises others to "deal with the issues that are right in front of you."

She provides an example of a small change in her practice, one that, for her, means the difference between "coming from a place of knowing" and simply doing as one is told:

> We have a textbook that we are testing . . . and one of the requirements was that we adhere to the textbook "with fidelity." I had to give it a chance because I'm required to. I have a preamble for the students: "We're reading this text, but I just know that there's something called critical reading and critical literacy. Know that the ideas expressed here are the author's ideas and doesn't mean you

have to take them as gospel. They are not gospel. You're allowed to agree or disagree with whatever you read." So I found myself doing that a lot because I was coming from a place of knowing as opposed to just saying, "This is our text. We are reading this today," and that's the end of it.

As Janet explains, the professional development she experienced through "reading and being aware through literature" made a difference in her practice and, by extension, in her students' development as critical readers.

Most importantly, Janet advocates for her students by helping them "navigate the system" in order to be successful while still being "their true selves." She describes her classroom as a space for students to "explore experiences." Drawing on her own experience to bridge the curriculum and students' experience is an important pedagogical tool that helps Janet achieve this goal of teaching students to navigate the system while being true to themselves.

Janet's "greatest concern" is academic success. She fears that, without it, students may "not be able to participate fully in the society that they are in." Thus, differentiating instruction is another important form of advocacy for Janet. For her, equity and access to the curriculum, as measured through standards, is at the heart of social-justice teaching. She "crafts assignments" in ways that are socially just because she recognizes that "how to get [students] there" (to meet the objective/standard) and "allowing them to arrive at the standard in different ways" is part of the "big picture."

She "gives [students] the tools that they need" for success by using "texts" or "avenues" that they are "comfortable using." While Janet's "small changes" may have big ripple effects in her classroom and in her students' academic successes, a larger, more transformational practice that she consistently employs is encouraging her students to use their home languages to accomplish goals in her classroom. She builds a multilingual community in her classroom to enhance academic success as she advocates for her students to write in their own languages. She calls this the "wiggle room" that students need to communicate well and learn.

As discussed in the chapter opening, action must move toward transformation of institutional policies and practices, resulting in changes that filter down into the everyday experiences of students currently experiencing inequities (Gorski & Swalwell, 2023). This pedagogical move is important, given the political contexts of English-only laws in many US public schools. For Janet, the act of teaching English is itself a form of advocacy:

> The act of teaching students English is activism and an act of social justice. You are empowering the students with the tools that they need to succeed in the society that they are in. There are just so many things stacked against them, but if they can at least get this one thing going, they'll be able to read whatever

letters are sent to them, go to a restaurant and read the menu, and be able to enjoy a meal in a place they otherwise would not have enjoyed if they did not have the language skills to do that. You're making their life better than it was before, and for their families too. It has a ripple effect in the community. So education itself, I think, is a form of activism, and especially when you're teaching ESL students because then you're helping them to be successful, not just for them, but also for their communities.

Janet employs an asset-based lens that envisions her students as "resilient," "strong," and "brave." She interacts with students from a place of deep empathy and care—this is reflected in her patient and responsive pedagogy. Several of her narratives focus on individual students and the ways that she worked to resolve situations that could easily have resulted in failing grades but that she assessed as "crises of confidence."

An asset-based pedagogical lens is one that highlights students' resources and strengths. Although assessment is a necessary part of teaching, it often focuses on what students cannot do or do not know rather than on what they can do or do know. Janet realizes that "those experiences [of refugeeism] taught them something about life, how to be tough and how to persevere and how to be resilient." At the same time, she recognizes that many students need time to adjust, usually much more than the current public-school system allows.

Because she knows students need time to adjust, Janet allows that low test scores may not necessarily mean a lack of "college readiness" or "that they can't perform well when they go to college." She sees her greatest challenge as "figuring out how to help when they're still at the high-school level" rather than relying on "remedial courses" from their chosen college.

Time is especially important for refugee students who risk "aging out" of the public school system. In Janet's state, students must leave when they turn twenty-one years old. She recounts many experiences of students whose documents are inaccurate, reflecting incorrect names and birth dates. She reports that many students are assigned a birth date upon entering the country. Janets explains as follows:

> So that really gets to me. I had a student the other day that according to her immigration documents, she is twenty-one or twenty-two, and therefore has to exit the public school system. But in reality, the girl is seventeen or something like that. So now her schooling has been cut short because of faulty documents and because if you're running away from rebels or whoever is coming to burn down your house, I mean, your birth certificate is not the thing that you're thinking about to get out of the house. You are running for your life. If they could get someone to, in those rooms when they're making those determinations, someone who speaks the language and can convey the correct date, then that would

really help. Because that girl was enjoying school. She was loving it. But then suddenly she can't go on anymore.

Janet laments that such experiences contribute to a lack of motivation. She also knows from her own experience that many of her students "come from very different places where age is not a determinant of your grade level." While Janet knows this is a policy issue that is beyond her control as a classroom teacher, she "wish[es] it would be different."

Janet understands that multiple barriers exist for her students. Her pedagogy is thus focused on, in her words, "navigating" those. When asked what her students need, Janet replied,

Some of them need confidence to know that they can do it, especially when it comes to postsecondary education and postsecondary opportunities. Some are hesitant to embrace them because they have so many other things that they have to consider that the people who were born here don't have to consider. They have to worry about, "If I move away, who's going to take care of my parents?"

Janet's realizations about her students' family lives are important. She refuses to rehash the myth of poverty. Instead, she recognizes generational wealth as an asset in progress. She continues, "Because a lot of them work in their homes and they contribute towards the bills, they don't have generational wealth to rely on. They're building it now and they're part of the people that are building that wealth." For Janet, the "family factor" is never a detriment or barrier, but a growing asset.

REFLECTION

This chapter examines the unique ways that Kay and Janet narrate themselves as socially just teachers and advocates. Kay, for example, reflects on a career of innovating responsive curricular shifts. She is currently campaigning for an influential political office. Janet is a self-described activist who teaches English through Swahili, her students' home language.

Both cite curiosity and continuing study as a key ingredient in their professional lives. This is important because research in schools reveals that resettled refugee youth appreciate teachers who seek to understand their stories and backgrounds, responsively support them in achieving academically, and enact flexible, responsive pedagogies that attend to each learner's experiences and goals (Oikonomidoy, 2010).

A key component of culturally relevant teaching is sociopolitical consciousness (Ladson-Billings, 2006). Kay shows us that, through her experiences, including actually getting out of teaching and away from the confines of school norms and policies, she has developed a much broader understanding of Somali culture and Islam. She now talks about inclusion at the table as a simple but profoundly difficult task.

In that her life experiences and identities align with those of her students in some ways, Janet teaches from a place of deep understanding, empathy, and care. However, for Janet, knowing and doing are two different things. She recognizes that, while she may know some things about her students' lives, supporting their academic success involves making incremental changes that may ripple out to have broader impacts.

An equity-literate educator possesses the ability to recognize, respond to, redress, actively cultivate, and sustain equity and justice (Gorski & Swalwell, 2015). Kay recognizes that action must move toward transformation of institutional policies and practices in order to filter down into the everyday experiences of communities—especially those of her former students and their families. Janet urges teachers to address "the issues in front of [them]." She envisions herself as part of a team of equity-oriented educators who, together, actively cultivate equity for refugee students through holistic individual attention and differentiated academic instruction.

In both stories, the structure of schooling itself limits opportunities for refugee students. Mora Mora (2021) writes, "Whilst everyone has the right to education (The United Nations General Assembly, 1966, art. 13), schooling is simply not enough for this right to be fulfilled" (p. 375). For Kay, whose classroom often felt like a "battleground," building community and designing a culturally relevant curriculum seemed an impossible task. It took years to create a responsive unit with which she was finally satisfied. However, her current political career allows her to work for equity and justice in broader and more impactful ways.

Janet, deeply aware of the barriers and challenges faced by her students, works tirelessly to create welcoming and safe spaces that allow her students the time they need to adjust to their new environments while attaining their goals. She often feels as if her work is unpaid and makes critical, often challenging, decisions about how to set boundaries between her personal life as a loving parent and her professional life as a caring teacher.

It seems that Kay and Janet both struggle with similar issues as public-school teachers in chronically underfunded schools where the needs of the newest and most marginalized students are not often a priority. Each embodies the role of the "lone hero" (Barret et al., 2011) in slightly different ways. Janet talks about the many adults in the building who work together and who are "keen on social-justice issues." Importantly, she sees herself as part of a team of like-minded educators supporting refugee students. At the same time, she recognizes personal limits and talks about the importance of self-care and setting personal boundaries.

Kay, on the other hand, often talks about herself as a teacher who, although with the support of her principal, must defend the music curriculum to parents. She feels supported by the EL teachers in the building but recognizes that, as a content-area specialist, she is on her own when it comes to curriculum. She relies on the internet to research Somali music. When the school district finally hired cultural navigators, she was able to better understand some of the parents' concerns, although language barriers remain an issue.

Finally, both talk about the centrality of their roles as women in teaching and politics. Motherhood is Janet's most important identity. She weaves this very personal responsibility into her teaching and talks about her students as if they are her own children. At the same time, she keenly feels the intense professional demands that limit her choices around caring for a family.

Kay, influenced by the civil rights movement, admires "three powerful women in her church" who were "intelligent, confident making decisions, speaking up in groups, and leading." She sees herself as a strong, curious, and open-minded former teacher and politician. In her own words, "It is time for women to be candidates." She is a determined and outspoken advocate for Somali and Muslim families in her community.

Kay and Janet are both equity literate and culturally relevant teachers who model possibilities. Although they come to teaching with vastly different life experiences and self-identities, they both draw on those experiences and identities as pedagogical resources. They reflect on their personal values and beliefs and how those inform their teaching for the benefit of their students. Most importantly, they work tirelessly building relationships with and advocating for refugee students and families.

REFERENCES

Barrett, S. E., Ford, D., & James, C. (2010). Beyond the lone hero: Providing supports for new teachers in high-needs schools. *Occasional Paper Series*, 2011 (25). doi: https://doi.org/10.58295/2375-3668.1085.

Bonilla-Silva, E. (2010). *Racism without racists: Color-blind racism and the persistence of racial inequality in the United States*. Rowman & Littlefield Publishers, Inc.

COE (2023). Characteristics of public school teachers. National Center for Education Statistics. https://nces.ed.gov/programs/coe/indicator/clr/public-school-teachers, accessed 6/14/23.

Delpit, L. (1995). *Other people's children: Cultural conflict in the classroom*. New Press.

Gorski, P., & Swalwell, K. (2015). Equity literacy for all. *Educational Leadership*, *72*(6), 34–40.

Gorski, P., & Swalwell, K. (2023). *Fix injustice, not kids, and other principles for transformative equity leadership*. Association for Supervision and Curriculum Development.

Kohli, R. (2011). Working to ensure safety, belonging and success for unaccompanied asylum-seeking children. *Child Abuse Review, 20*, 311–23.

Ladson-Billings, G. (2006). Yes, but how do we do it? In J. Landsman, & C. Lewis (Eds.), *White teachers/diverse classrooms: A guide to building inclusive schools, promoting high expectations, and eliminating racism*. Stylus.

McIntyre, J. & Abrams, F. (2021). *Refugee education: Theorising practice in schools*. Routledge.

Mora Mora, M. E. (2021). Refugee voices on active citizenship and social justice: Life stories from the field. In Isabel Maria Gomez Nieto (Ed.), *Promoting social justice for immigrants and refugees through active citizenship and intercultural education*. IGI Global.

Noddings, N. (1984). *Caring, a feminine approach to ethics & moral education*. University of California Press.

Noddings, N. (1995). Teaching themes of care. *The Phi Delta Kappan, 76*(2), 675–79.

Oikonomidoy, E. (2010). Zooming into the school narratives of refugee students. *Multicultural Perspectives, 12*(2), 74–80.

Roxas, K. C. (2011). Creating communities: Working with refugee students in classrooms. *Democracy & Education, 19*(2), 1–8.

Yosso, T. J. (2005). Whose culture has capital? A critical race theory discussion of community cultural wealth. *Race, Ethnicity, and Education, 8*(1), 69–91.

Chapter 7

Recommendations for Supporting Educators of Refugee and Displaced Students

The authors cannot stress enough how grateful they are to the teachers who shared their personal and professional stories with us. They are changemakers. They reflect and resist. They respond to limited resources while drawing on their own personal identities, experiences, and resources as reserves. They foster community and advocate for themselves and their students. By agreeing to talk with us about these issues, they demonstrate an admirable vulnerability and openness that does not come easily.

The prism perspective allows us to agree on a single truth and explore it from many angles. Consider, for example, the truth that refugee and displaced students are an underserved population of students. Or that their teachers are under-supported and under-resourced. Each truth paradoxically contains many truths. When a single truth passes through the prism, it can be broken apart and examined as many perspectives on truth, as white light becomes a spectrum of colors.

The teachers featured here share an asset-based lens, not only for their students but also for themselves and other teachers. Positioning teachers as knowledgeable and agentive is particularly important within a sociopolitical climate of teacher bashing and de-professionalization that currently drives a high number of teachers out of the classroom every year. This book echoes a call for teachers to recognize and honor their own knowledge and to advocate for equitable conditions for themselves and their students.

That being said, ideologies of Whiteness seep in, even in the face of concerted archeology of self. US schools, as microcosms of the society that produces them, are steeped in Whiteness. Critical race and refugee theories say that identity and experience *do* matter and that we *must* listen to those who are marginalized. Although all but one of the teachers identify as White, and none have refugee backgrounds, the authors stress that their experiences not only matter but also serve as valuable leverage in developing the kind of critical consciousness that may be our best resource for supporting refugee and displaced students.

The remainder of this chapter will focus on recommendations arising from each previous chapter. As noted, the authors value the prismatic approach in which multiple voices, identities, experiences, and perspectives are brought to bear on the examination of the issues. On one level, each chapter is a deep dive into the experiences, knowledge, and beliefs of individual classroom teachers. On another level, the chapters are filled with stories co-constructed between a participant and a researcher/author, each of whom comes to the inquiry with her own experiences, knowledge, and beliefs.

The recommendations offered here reflect the unique perspectives that the authors bring to the study based on their diverse professional roles. These range from classroom teacher, to building-level administrator, to district-level administrator, to teacher educator, to community consultant. Each of the following sets of recommendations wears the hat, so to speak, of a professional educator in a particular role. They are presented here in the order that the chapters appeared in the book.

RECOMMENDATIONS FROM CHAPTER 2. CRITICAL CONSCIOUSNESS AND WHITE SAVIORISM IN TEACHER NARRATIVES

Public education in the United States is a twofold embrace in which school-district leadership and classroom teaching are both the framers and the deliverers. In this section, the authors offer encouragement for bringing district leadership practices in relation to teacher efficacy to the forefront. It is important to acknowledge the tensions in this pairing. Often, the school district is the system against which classroom teachers might see themselves pitted.

Frequently, classroom teachers feel themselves pushing up against administration as they seek resources for their students. At the same time, districts control professional-development opportunities and provide training that helps guard against teachers feeling that they are alone and need to fight for equity on their own.

In a politically charged landscape, school districts can empower learners by empowering their teachers. Considering Chloe and Jill's deep desire to *help*, teachers need a safe space to ask for help and work through their insecurities. High ethical and moral expectations for teachers to *help* come from many directions. However, the authors agree that teachers need *help*, too. Recent social and political changes, especially after the pandemic, have created a demanding classroom space.

Teachers need autonomy and anonymity. They need a space where they can inquire about their ignorance, learn the truth, and express without opprobrium. This could be an online or in-person space where they can stay curious and free of judgment. Teachers like Chloe and Jill, who identify as White and who do not come from refugee backgrounds themselves, are determined to provide learners and their families with the best possible outcomes in life; however, race and culture create invisible double standards that even the most well-intentioned teachers are unable to consider.

At the same time, district leadership should place weight on creating policies that are explicitly intolerant of harmful language and outdated teaching practices. For example, districts should demand that educators provide choice and diverse entry points so that displaced learners can navigate their own learning. In addition, accountability measures can be improved.

One example is an inclusive decision-making framework that comes in the form of a checklist. The framework provides a more in-depth consideration and reflection on potential and unintended consequences of all participatory decision-making processes. This framework has the potential to increase transparency, accountability, equity, and influence. It is an easily applicable and holistic model of an inclusive participatory decision-making process.

The framework is simple but interrogative, making room for more in-depth thought processes. It also clearly defines the subject of inclusivity, the *who*. In this case, the framework brings to the forefront how highly affected students and other stakeholders experience additional burdens or barriers in the pursuit of educational opportunities.

The tool is simple enough to apply to decisions at the leadership, classroom, and curriculum-development levels. Most importantly, the framework can be envisioned as an extension of the mission, vision, and values of the school district. The framework reorganizes four affirmative sentences around inclusion into interrogative questions:

- Affirmative: Our mission is to advance serving highly affected students.
- Question: Does this decision advance serving highly affected students?
- Affirmative: We value additional perspective in enhancing the educational experiences of ALL learners.
- Question: Does this decision need additional perspectives before finalizing?
- Affirmative: Our vision is to improve access for students and their families.
- Question: Does this decision improve access for students and their families?

- Affirmative: We will encourage collaboration and partnership to produce positive outcomes for learners.
- Question: Does this decision encourage collaboration and partnership?

The framework has a fifth question, a critical one that demands a thoughtful consideration of the unforeseen.

- What are the unintended consequences of this decision? AND what considerations need to be made to mitigate these consequences?

In practice, decisions often fail to bring about one hundred percent positive outcomes for highly affected learners, creating some unintended negative feelings, resentment, distrust, etc. The final question requires a thoughtful consideration of such and possible mitigation efforts. In summary, each question reviews and empirically extends any district's decision-making process into diversity, equity, and inclusion.

RECOMMENDATIONS FROM
CHAPTER 3. CHANGEMAKING AND RESISTING

In this section, the authors offer words of hope for classroom teachers who dare to become a threat to inequity within their personal and professional zones of influence. Even on an individual level, teachers can act as changemakers by remaining open to alternative solutions and adapting creatively to changing school climates. They can consider alternative curricular materials as resources that are responsive to students' experiences and knowledge. They can be imaginative about creating new models and opportunities.

Teachers can practice agency independently and within collaborative spaces and recognize how both can be advantageous to changemaking. They might leverage opportunities to take leadership, but also maintain cooperation with colleagues who are prepared to learn from and with them in creative experimentation. This openness and vulnerability may allow changemaking to grow and spread beyond individual classrooms.

Educators can practice resistance in order to support refugee newcomers by slowing, refusing, and negating norms that disadvantage their students. By resisting established structure and roles, educators may find liminal spaces as alternatives. Resisting existing roles may be a powerful way to elicit justice. When teachers acknowledge the privileges, power, and authority they hold, and work to resist their impact, they may be able to better understand the experiences of refugee and displaced newcomers.

Educators can resist by working to recast individuals in roles that traditionally uphold privilege and power structures. By reclaiming and reestablishing positional roles, educators can resist normative structures. They can also resist by refusing to accept limits of assumptions or resources. By working around limited resources, like seeking new tools, teachers can resist the externally imposed limitations of their curriculum.

Educators can also resist colleagues' and communities' limiting perspectives that may shadow their work. Instead, teachers can dispute these limits in words and actions. Teachers need to feel empowered to do more of what they know is helpful and good. Norms may not reflect what teachers know about themselves and their refugee and displaced students.

Being a changemaker allows teachers to be flexible and adaptive in their work. It allows them to work intuitively and inquire about what could be. Teachers who practice resistance are able to disengage with the system in which they work and instead imagine a way to do more of what they know works for their students. Although teachers may feel limited by systems outside their classrooms, changemakers and resisters can imagine new ways to do more of what works.

RECOMMENDATIONS FROM CHAPTER 4. EMPATHY AND AGENCY

From a building-level administrative lens, the authors offer the following recommendations, based on Steven's and Naomi's experiences. Given that teacher education and early career mentorship programs emphasize self-reflection, we know that teachers who engage in self-reflection are often better positioned for adaptability and in their work with students. We also know that individuals who have a greater understanding of themselves feel more empowered within their various contexts. This study has extended those notions into social-justice teaching and teacher agency.

Educators can more intentionally practice radical empathy and social-justice teaching when they can dive into a purposeful archeology of self (Sealey Ruiz, 2022). School leaders have a responsibility to displaced and refugee students to employ teachers who actively challenge their own stereotypes and beliefs. Opportunities must be provided for teachers to be led through the vulnerable process of uncovering how their own histories and biases infuse their classrooms. This requires shared trust and the development of radical empathy.

Teachers and school administrators can demonstrate radical empathy and social justice by providing opportunities for displaced and refugee students to be seen and heard. Whether those opportunities are curricular, co-curricular, or in the community, refugee and displaced students need a means to have their voices, backgrounds, traditions, and sense of self recognized and valued in their new contexts.

Curriculum should be made available for all students to see the experience of refugee and displaced students mirrored or paralleled. Pedagogies should be employed that capitalize on the strengths these students bring to the space. Extended activities should both celebrate and stretch the gifts and capabilities these students have and show how they bring additional perspective and value to the community.

School administrators should develop an understanding of the educational systems in their students' original nations and regions to develop a bridge for refugee and displaced students in their new contexts. Through that understanding, school administrators could develop more appropriate, clear, and effective transition programs to support refugee and displaced students and their families. Such transition programs should not only address enrollment of children into schools but also purposefully assess student needs and address family understandings of what school is like in the current situation.

Families should be actively engaged throughout the transition process as collaborative members in the children's education. Teachers should actively work to practice their agency within their schools and communities. We know that agency "depends on structures and cultures which can either foster or suspend it" (Pantic, 2015, p. 763), so it is important for school administrators to nurture the degrees of power teachers are given in their various roles within the school context.

Teachers should be able to share their commitments to promoting social justice and to pushing back against inequality, discrimination, bias, and stereotypes without reprisal. Teachers should be encouraged to develop understandings and practices that build their knowledge and awareness about social-justice issues related to their school. They should be allowed to enact their purpose and competence in school development, policymaking, and collaboration in the system.

RECOMMENDATIONS FROM CHAPTER 5. VULNERABILITY AND OVERCOMING CHALLENGES

Recommendations from Chapter 5 focus on the challenges of the pandemic and how teachers might overcome the myriad of challenges that have arisen as a result. This set of recommendations focuses specifically on technology resources and how they might be leveraged to improve students' and teachers' experiences.

First is more usable professional development for teachers. Current training does not support teachers in providing a safe and positive learning environment for this student population. For instance, responsible for her students' language arts, reading, and spelling grades, Emily expressed her frustration with the lack of instructional time. She wished she could be in two places at once to support and help her students, referring to this as a "dream."

In another example, there seems to be a misunderstanding by many in the school about the unique needs of refugee and displaced students. Collaboration is one way for teachers and administrators to get a better understanding of students' needs. For instance, Emily proposed that schools often misdiagnosed ESL students and that, when collaboration occurred, there could have been better communication among different constituents, such as counselors, EL teachers, content teachers, and administrators.

Moreover, the COVID-19 pandemic has affected teachers' work and student involvement. Society must examine the intersection of social justice and educational technology to determine its potential for justice. The pandemic and school closures have impacted students from all socioeconomic backgrounds due to challenges in remote learning, technology infrastructure issues, lack of hands-on help, and family-related factors. To improve student engagement, teachers should collaborate with professional networks, maintain open communication with families, and plan interactive activities for students.

Participants' narratives highlight the importance of keeping families informed about changes in expectations and procedures. Establishing school-home relationships for resilience is crucial for maintaining a safe learning environment. Regularly connecting with families and providing participation options address students' social-emotional needs and build communities that enhance student engagement and achievement. Multiple platforms should be used to communicate information, particularly in native languages.

High-quality pedagogical and technical preparation and professional development are needed. Technology, remote learning, teacher training, support, and retention are also crucial. Social justice is essential for citizens to feel happy, fulfilled, and content in society, ensuring equal contribution from all members. Districts should hire teachers like Emily, Nicole, and others who value their students and families' efforts and cultures. These teachers have big hearts, love teaching, and feel pride when families realize their children's potential and need for support regarding their social-emotional well-being.

RECOMMENDATIONS FROM CHAPTER 6. BUILDING CLASSROOM COMMUNITY AND ADVOCACY

This final set of recommendations offers suggestions for teacher education. These stories underscore the obvious and well-known urgent issue that teaching is a woefully under-supported and under-resourced profession. Few teachers would disagree with what these teachers make abundantly clear—they feel underpaid, exhausted, and often like "lone heroes," especially in a post-COVID world. Teachers of the most vulnerable populations, like refugee students, feel these pressures even more intensely.

The authors recommend that teacher preparation be conceived of as a continual process, one that centers the evolving issues and realities of students' lives in the schools and communities where teachers themselves actually live and teach. Learning to teach, as is clear from Kay and Janet's stories, is a lifelong process that evolves in response to the rapidly changing social, economic, and political contexts of global shift. The question might be "learning to teach whom?" rather than "learning to teach what (content)?" This kind of teacher education would require significant and ongoing investment and political will.

Being prepared as a teacher means being constantly responsive to who students are. It is a given that innovations in curriculum, assessment, standards, language instruction, and pedagogical resources will continuously be needed. As Kay and Janet experienced firsthand, we can no longer assume what it will mean to prepare teachers for classrooms in rural, suburban, or urban settings as if these descriptors represent a stable meaning. In fact, conceptions of urbanity are changing and will continue to change. Instead, teacher preparation needs a much broader, experiential foundation.

Teacher education does, in theory, provide resources and ways of thinking that promote openness, diversity, and curiosity. However, it seems that a sharper attention to developing new teachers' sociopolitical consciousness alongside specific pedagogical strategies and skills would be beneficial. Janet explains in her own words:

> What I realize is that [the classroom] is just a small slice of society. Whatever goes on out there [in the larger society] goes on here. So whatever good, whatever evil, whatever stuff you find out there, don't think that the school is immune to that. It is not immune to that. So be prepared to deal with the good and the bad and don't be surprised. The ones that I feel for are probably the university graduates—the younger student teachers. I think having them exposed to different settings for student teaching would be great so that they can have an idea of what to expect. And also being prepared for if students are performing

below grade level and strategies. And also being prepared on how to deal with large populations of ESL students.

Individual teachers have very specific sets of experiences, attitudes, beliefs, values, and skills. This means that teacher education might focus even more on beginning with where teachers are in their experiences. They must recognize that it is engagement with other perspectives that allows for fuller understanding.

Far from being neutral, conceptions of community are loaded with personal and social associations and meanings, or ideologies. Ideologies undergird Kay's and Janet's narratives, as they do all narratives. Telling and reflecting on teaching stories offers hope. If we can deconstruct our stories, we can construct new narratives and change our lives and, by extension, the lives of those around us.

One example of an experience designed to address issues rediscovered in this study is a community dinner organized for culturally diverse teachers, students, and families at the research site described in Chapter 4. With the support of Spencer Foundation Grant funding, the authors worked with a local nonprofit organization to sponsor a community conversation and educational meeting. In this particular case, parents, administrators, teachers, and students gathered at a public elementary school to eat specially prepared Dominican and Puerto Rican food and to share and hear stories of survival after Hurricane Maria devastated Puerto Rico in 2017.

One goal was to help teachers reframe their views of families as "unstable" or parents as "contributing" to the instabilities caused by displacement. Another was to provide a forum for families to share their survivor stories. Parents were positioned as the experts on their experiences and the needs of their children. They created a presentation retelling the experience and highlighting their strengths. From this emic perspective, teachers and administrators were allowed a glimpse of how the experience drew out the best in their students and their families and how this community grew because of it.

CONCLUSION

Although this book is not an edited collection, neither is it the product of a cohesive voice. It is an attempt to come together and make sense of many perspectives. Narrative inquiry is both analysis of narratives and narrative analysis. In other words, we come together to bring frameworks (identities and experiences) that sometimes align, sometimes contradict, sometimes support, and sometimes talk over each other. This creates a cacophony representative of educational research in general. When we attempt to streamline to cut down on the "noise" and create a single truth, we necessarily cut something out.

Kumashiro (2022) asks us to write into the tensions of our work. For example, we know teachers are a decisive element in seeking to transform educational inequities, yet they frequently lack the necessary knowledge and skills to address the needs of their students. There is a tension in the idea that we can know something about teaching by telling stories. The authors recognize that they make broad, perhaps even sweeping, claims about these teachers' practices. They did not observe the teachers, nor did they talk with students or other stakeholders.

The authors do know that all of the teachers valued the interview experience. They said that they felt listened to and, most importantly, that they felt *heard*. The authors suggest that this kind of narrative reflexivity offers space for learning and growth. It is well understood that teachers' practices are crafted in response to the contexts in which they find themselves, and pedagogies are mediated by personal values, beliefs, and cultural orientations. Teachers who question their own biases and examine deficit views can reimagine their own and their students' strengths, skills, and needs to improve instruction.

A unique aspect of this narrative inquiry is how the researchers' identities and experiences are woven into the research narrative. The study represents a collaboration between researchers and participants, over time, in a place or series of places, and in social interaction. As narrative scholars, the authors are aware of layers of narratives and stories nested within stories—those of the participants as well as those of the researchers.

Educators are refugee and displaced students' best resources for creating socially just and equitable classroom spaces. As illustrated here, this endeavor is complex and perhaps even an elusive goal. These teachers show us how they aspire toward critical consciousness. Rather than offering stories with coherent themes and messages, they offer paradox and nuance. These are stories of vulnerability, empathy, White saviorism, agency, advocacy, change-making, and resistance.

Finally, we offer the idea that "love without truth is not love. Truth without love is not truth" (Dekel & Dekel, 2019, p. 138). Social-justice pedagogy is inherently rooted in love and truth. To locate truth is to invite and honor many perspectives. Love must be accompanied by a critical stance that makes visible both the light and the shadows.

Critical perspectives on social justice and equity, especially for refugee and displaced students in US schools, are more urgently needed now than ever. Who better to inform what we know than the teachers who have dedicated their professional lives to advocating for these students? We offer these stories, and accept them, with both love and understanding of the nature of truth, which is multifaceted.

REFERENCES

Dekel, N. & Dekel, G. (2019). *The energy book*. Natalie and Gil Dekel.

Kumashiro, K. (2022, May 5–8). Writing Workshop and Retreat: Writing for Movement Building. Wai'anae, HI.

Pantic, N. (2015). A model for the study of teacher agency for social justice. *Teachers and Teaching, 21(6)*, 759–78.

Sealey-Ruiz, Y. (2022). An archaeology of self for our times. *English Journal, 111*(5), 21–26.

Index

advocacy, 6, 8, 16, 37, 47, 87, 89, 95, 99–100: self-, 65, 76
agency, 8, 13, 16, 26, 41, 48, 51, 59–66, 110–12: teacher, 17, 52–53, 58
archeology of self, 17, 66, 107, 111

belonging, 16, 34, 56, 61–62, 88, 97, 98

changemakers, 37, 41, 47, 49, 110, 111
community-as-place, 88
community building, 87–88, 91, 97
community cultural capital, 22, 27, 88
counternarratives, 15
COVID-19 pandemic, 1, 8, 30, 40, 41, 57, 64, 65, 69, 70, 76, 82, 83, 109, 113, 114
critical consciousness-raising, 15, 16, 21, 69
critical pedagogy, 14
critical reflection, 16, 17, 51, 66: self-reflection, 8, 16, 51
critical race theory, 15, 16, 59
cultural capital, 22, 25–27, 88
cultural navigator, 94, 95, 104
culturally relevant, xi, 13, 14–17, 29, 88, 92, 93, 99, 102–4

deficit, 12, 26, 49, 64, 73, 92, 116

displaced students or learners, 2–8, 12–15, 25–34, 45, 47–49, 54, 61, 62–66, 70, 83–85, 107–12, 116: Muslim, 25; from Puerto Rico, 51, 56
dysconscious racism, 23

empathy, 8, 51–66, 111,
equity literacy, 13, 89, 91

Hurricane Maria, 8, 12, 115

internally displaced, 12

liberation, 15, 21: pedagogy, 30
"lone hero," 89, 93, 94, 99, 103, 114

meritocracy, 22, 30, 32
meta-narratives, 22, 23, 35, 43
microcosms, 21, 88, 107
Muslim, 6, 23–25, 46, 71, 79, 82, 91–93

newcomer, 37, 41–49, 64, 110

pedagogical entrepreneurship, 37–41, 46
prism perspective, 107. *See also* prismatic approach
prismatic approach, 108. *See also* prism perspective

Puerto Rico, 12, 51, 56, 62, 115

radical empathy, 52, 53, 57, 66, 111
RefugeeCrit, 15, 16
refugees, 12–13, 15–17, 39–40, 61, 77, 92, 96
Resistance, 38, 42, 48, 49, 110, 111, 116

social-emotional, 81, 84, 113
sociopolitical consciousness, 21, 88, 102, 114
Somali(a), 13, 28–31, 39, 46, 90–95, 103–4

systemic: inequities, 15, 17; injustices, 13; issues, 58

teacher narratives, 7–8, 21, 25
trauma-informed, 81, 84

vulnerability, 8, 17, 30, 69, 70, 72–73, 76, 79, 81–82, 83, 107, 110

Whiteness, 22–24, 33, 42, 43, 107
White saviorism, 8, 15, 16, 21–23, 26, 31–33, 34

About the Authors

Terri L. Rodriguez, PhD, is a professor of education and a former secondary English teacher at the College of St. Benedict and St. John's University in St. Joseph, Minnesota. Her research explores issues of social justice, equity, and diversity in schools.

Laura Mahalingappa, PhD, is an associate professor of applied linguistics and language education at the University of Maryland. Her teaching and research focus on the language and education and teacher preparation for marginalized learners.

Ayan Omar, MA, is the Director of Equity Services and a former high-school teacher at St. Cloud Area School District in St. Cloud, Minnesota. Her efforts in educational equity and community advocacy create improved connections and informed opportunities for a growing diverse community in Central Minnesota.

Lauren Ergen, MA, teaches English to multilingual students at Apollo High School in Saint Cloud, Minnesota. Her students are primarily individuals who recently arrived in the United States and who have limited or interrupted formal education in their background.

Odessa Ghassa-Khalil, EdD, is a community cultural consultant in Pittsburgh, Pennsylvania. She completed her doctorate in educational technology and leadership from Duquesne University and has been an Arabic teacher and educational advocate.

Jennifer L. Meagher, EdD, is currently a director of student teaching at the College of Saint Benedict and Saint John's University and was formerly a middle- and high-school principal and English teacher. Her professional focus is on the development of educators who tap into their identity and values to teach equitably, authentically, and lovingly.

www.ingramcontent.com/pod-product-compliance
Lightning Source LLC
Chambersburg PA
CBHW030144240426
43672CB00005B/260